D1595778

The Crown Prince Rudolf

His Mysterious Life After Mayerling

The Crown Prince Rudolf

His Mysterious Life After Mayerling

by

Dr. Enrique Lardé

HONNI SOIT QUI MAL Y PENSE...

DORRANCE PUBLISHING CO., INC.
PITTSBURGH, PENNSYLVANIA 15222

All Rights Reserved
Copyright © 1994 by Enrique Roberto Lardé
No part of this book may be reproduced or transmitted
in any form or by any means, electronic or mechanical,
including photocopying, recording, or by any information
storage and retrieval system without permission in
writing from the publisher.

ISBN # 0-8059-3580-0
Printed in the United States of America

First Printing

For information or to order additional books, please write:
Dorrance Publishing Co., Inc.
643 Smithfield Street
Pittsburgh, Pennsylvania 15222
U.S.A.

TABLE OF CONTENTS

VI. ONLY THE MEMORY REMAINS

1860
Back row, from left to right:
Franz Joseph, Ferdinand Maximilian Joseph, Charlotte,
Louis Victor, Karl Ludwig.

Front row, from left to right:
Rudolf, Elizabeth, Gisela, Sophia, Ferdinand I.

Amelie Arthés died 17 January 1911.
Photograph dated 19 January 1911; two days later.

Standing, left to right: Zelie, Carlos, Alice, Luis, Marie, and José.
Seated, left to right: Coralie, Guillermo Manuel, Jorge, and Enrique.

The day George Lardé died, 1903
Clockwise from top, center: Enrique Lardé, Carlos Lardé,
Alice Lardé, Luis Lardé, Zelie Lardé,
Maria Lardé, Coralie Lardé, and Jorge Lardé.

The Crown Prince Rudolf

Enrique Lardé—28 November 1917
From graduation photograph.

The Crown Prince Rudolf

Enrique Lardé—November 1930

The Archduke Rudolf von Hapsburg
Copyright © 1981 Enrique Lardé

Graduation photograph, 28 November 1917.
Enrique Lardé, Luis Edmundo Vázquez, and Tomás Mena.

George Lardé (1859 - 1903)
Amelie Arthés (1868 - 1911)
Photograph, 13 March 1891

Wedding photograph, November 24, 1930
Dr. and Mrs. Enrique Lardé
Miss Abby Lardé (daughter of Dr. Luis Lardé)

Dr. and Mrs. Enrique Lardé shortly after 60th wedding
anniversary, November 24, 1990

PREFACE

This memoir is not just one more book about Archduke Rudolf and the tragedy of Mayerling. Many books have been written on the subject but all are more or less false, and almost all more or less defamatory. The passion for subterfuge has led even to the falsification of documents and the publication of a doctored photograph supposedly of the dead body of Archduke Rudolf recumbent, his head bandaged to suggest that the dressing covers the nonexistent bullet wound. But at Mayerling, whatever may be said, no one died.

The tragedy of Mayerling assumed the proportions it did because of the endless succession of calumnies heaped upon a man remarkable for his intelligence, culture, purposes, great energy, and lofty standards.

The tragedy was the result of collusion between the clergy and the reactionary circles in the Habsburg Empire, who saw their interests threatened by the reforms whose possibility the Archduke envisaged for some indefinite future.

Officially, the Archduke committed suicide. But in fact he simply left Austria for a remote country and adopted the pseudonym "Justo Armas." He settled eventually in El Salvador where he could live in tranquility, recognized by no one.

During the tragedy of Mayerling the Archduke gave his word to keep his identity a secret for the rest of his life, and he kept the secret as much as his heart allowed. He was an Austrian named Justo Armas, so his passport testified. But in El Salvador he revealed the secret of his identity and the facts about Mayerling to one person and one person only. This he did for reasons entirely just and easy to understand, after solemn assurances that the secret would not be divulged.

In the capital city San Salvador, the Archduke fell in love with Doña Amelie Arthés de Lardé. And the only male child of the Archduke was born. That son of the Crown Prince is Dr. Enrique Rafael Lardé Arthés, author of this memoir. And if the Prince revealed his identity to my mother, it was clearly because he intended that I, his only son, should be told in due course.

My mother kept the secret of Don Justo's identity, as he desired, until she was on her deathbed. I also kept the secret even as she had urged me. But now, His Majesty the Emperor Francis Joseph and all of his generation being dead, and dead Don Justo Armas, the truth can hurt no one. I think I can now speak up, especially since at my age, being an octogenarian, no one can profit from harassing me.

When Don Justo Armas arrived in El Salvador he took lodgings in the Europa Hotel, which was owned by my mother and adopted father, Doña Amelie Arthés de Lardé and Don Jorge Lardé, and was warmly received there. Through my parents the Archduke gained admission into Salvadoran society. Don Justo adjusted rapidly to life in his new country.

My mother's words at her deathbed, repeating what the Archduke had told her, have been with me all my life and have allowed me to untangle the historical contradictions and obviously-manufactured lies and incongruities that have appeared about the Mayerling tragedy.

In her widely-known Political Testament, her Majesty the empress Maria Theresia (1717-1780), heiress to Habsburg succession and considered the 'universal and first mother of her peoples,' said the following: "With complete tranquility and pleasure, I would have even abandoned my whole right to rule and surrendered to my enemies, had Divine Providence so willed and had I believed it my duty or the best policy for my lands." The words of this extraordinary Empress express the Habsburg spirit of sacrificing personal and family interests to the welfare of their subjects. Emperor Francis Joseph sacrificed his family sentiments for what he thought were the best interests of his subjects. And Archduke Rudolf renounced all future claims as crown prince in the name of what the government thought best for the Empire. The governing principle of the Habsburg was to serve the nation. Such service implies great personal sacrifices that commoners do not always understand. In truth, as it has been said, the imperial crown is a crown of thorns.

After I had finished writing the first part of this memoir, my son Don Enrique R. Lardé, who had been zealous in his assistance, told me the work needed some account of the environment surrounding Don Justo Armas, that is, the circles in which he moved in El Salvador. That is indeed quite important for understanding the later, enigmatic years of the Archduke. I hesitated both from fear that the reader might not find entertaining an account of the particulars of my family and my wife's family, and from the possibility that the reader would interpret it as a show of personal pride, however justifiable it might be. But if all reference to our parents and ancestry is omitted, the description of the Archduke's new milieu would be much too incomplete. So in order that the later life of the Crown Prince might be well understood and aptly judged, I have found myself obliged to enter into those particulars. As a result, this memoir is as informative about my homeland, El Salvador, as it is of the House of Austria, when the history of that House was not only the history of Europe, but much more. I will, therefore, discuss:

1. What really happened at Mayerling.
2. The simulated burials of Baroness Maria Vetsera and the Archduke.
3. The slanders directed against the Crown Prince.
4. Why the Archduke ended up in El Salvador.
5. Why he adopted the pseudonym "Justo Armas."
6. How the Archduke was shipwrecked in the Straits of Magellan.
7. Why Empress Elizabeth, his mother, was assassinated.
8. The social environment found by the Archduke in El Salvador.

And may God forgive my having so delayed disclosure of the facts about the life of the Crown Prince, the Archduke Rudolf, after he did not commit suicide at Mayerling. But now I have at last made that disclosure and feel my conscience clear before the memory of Don Justo (to whom it was most due), before those whose position entitles them to known the truth, and before God.

I have taken pains in being as accurate as possible, and in the case of names, have used the formal names used by the people involved and the titles proper to them. Thus Doña Adriana Cabrolier Arthés would in English usage be Adriana Cabrolier. Arthés is her mother's last name, which in Spanish is always added at the end. Her mother was Doña Gabriela Arthés de Cabrolier; that is, she was married to Mr. Camilo Cabrolier. General Maximiliano Hernández Martínez should technically be called General Hernández, but since he is universally known as General Martínez, we must follow tradition and use, incorrectly, his mother's last name. I have chosen to write Rudolf instead of Rudolph, and Maria Theresia with an "i" since she liked the thirteen letters in her name.

I. The Archduke Rudolf

From Vienna to El Salvador

*A*rchduke Rudolf von Habsburg, only son of the emperor Francis Joseph, adopted the pseudonym "Justo Armas" after the tragedy of Mayerling, where he had allegedly committed suicide. He vanished from Austria on January 29, 1889, and arrived in El Salvador in September 1898 after surviving shipwreck in the Straits of Magellan. Why did it take so long for the Archduke to get from Vienna to his destination? Where was he during those ten years? Why did he always walk barefoot and why El Salvador of all places?

Since the turn of the century, Salvadoran society has known exactly why Don Justo always went barefoot, and known it because he himself explained it on his arrival. When the ship in which Don Justo traveled was crossing the Straits of Magellan, a violent storm with high winds swept the region; it foundered and was sunk. Don Justo somehow clung to one of the planks that remained afloat among the debris of the wreckage. In his anguish, in freezing wind and icy waters, and facing an all but certain death, Don Justo vowed to the Virgin that, if saved, he would walk barefoot forever after. The Virgin granted the miracle and Don Justo kept his word.

A small fisherboat chanced by the spot where Don Justo kept himself floating, took him aboard, and carried him ashore. After the shipwreck, the Archduke would presumably have been taken to a fisherman's hut and tended to carefully while he recuperated from the trauma caused by the shipwreck. One would imagine him repaying those who rescued him under such desperate circumstances by pitching in with his labor. He benefitted from a solid dose of field work in a remote region of Argentina, and henceforth was a hearty vigorous man who developed broad shoulders. Afterwards, he continued his route northwards through the Argentinian Pampas.

When he had managed to make good his losses and put together the moneys needed to go onward, the Archduke took ship, probably at Valparaíso, Chile, heading once more for his destination. The government of His Imperial Majesty, Francis Joseph, would have been informed by the Austrian Consul at the port of embarcation that Don Justo Armas had taken ship for El Salvador. The Emperor was doubtless also notified that the Archduke went barefoot. And although the report was kept secret, it doubtless must have reached the ears of the empress Elizabeth, Rudolf's mother, who was at the time in a hotel on the shores of Lake Geneva.

The Archduke Was Recognized

In those days, when the Archduke came to El Salvador, the only hotel in the city was the Europa Hotel, whose proprietors were my parents, Don Jorge Lardé and Doña Amelie Arthés de Lardé. The Archduke, who no longer made use of his titles of nobility and now known as "Justo Armas," fell in love with Doña Amelie Arthés de Lardé, and the first and only male child of the Archduke was born.

I am that child, Dr. Enrique Rafael Lardé Arthés, author of this memoir, son of the Crown Prince, and adopted son of Don Jorge Lardé, from whom I took my surname. My father Don Jorge knew me to be the carnal son of Don Justo Armas, but chose to adopt me as his son, as will later be explained. My godfather likewise, the young lieutenant in the French army who later became General Henri Giraud (1879-1949), knew me to be the son of Don Justo, and knew Don Justo to be Archduke Rudolf. So did my godmother Doña Adriana Cabrolier Arthés. They knew not from Justo Armas, however.

It became known that Don Justo was the Archduke Rudolf because the Austrian Consul, who had known him amid ancestral opulence in his homeland, recognized him barefoot in El Salvador.

The Consul in San Salvador recognized him at first sight, and discussed the event in private with his staff. He could not understand why the Crown Prince, who was thought dead, was walking barefoot in El Salvador. The event caused quite a commotion in the office. Most likely the Consul would have received instructions from Francis Joseph's government about the expected arrival in El Salvador of an Austrian citizen named Justo Armas. But it seems the Consul never imagined that that Austrian citizen would be the Archduke, let alone that he would be barefoot. As always happens, the secret quietly spread until all Salvadoran society of the time was in on it. Despite this, Don Justo never of himself disclosed his identity to anyone, except to one person only, as I shall discuss later on.

The Archduke Did Not Commit Suicide

he Austrian Consul communicated to His Majesty's Imperial Government that his son the Archduke had arrived in El Salvador under the name of Justo Armas. The Austrian government requested the Salvadoran government to keep it informed about the activities of the Archduke, and asked in particular that the identity of Don Justo Armas be kept confidential. The Salvadoran government complied faithfully with that obligation. It never publicly divulged that Don Justo Armas was none other than the Archduke Rudolf. But important persons in the Ministry of Foreign Relations of El Salvador have confirmed to me privately that Don Justo Armas was the Archduke Rudolf. It was natural for them to tell me, but I do not think that they disclosed the secret to anyone else. Of course, everyone in El Salvador remembers Don Justo Armas, and not a few became aware of the secret.

The dossier relative to the life and alleged death of Archduke Rudolf was extracted from the Austrian archives of state the day of his alleged death or soon thereafter. Therefore there exist no official documents concerning the Archduke's decisions about his titles and hereditary rights, his adoption of a pseudonym to conceal his identity, and his promise never to return to his beloved homeland.

Officially, the Archduke committed suicide. In reality, he adopted another name and left Austria. But in El Salvador he revealed himself to one single person as the Crown Prince, Archduke Rudolf, son of His Imperial Majesty, Francis Joseph, Emperor of Austria and Apostolic King of Hungary, and direct descendant of the most noble Empress Maria Theresia and also of Charles V, the Great, over whose vast dominions the sun never set.

The Crown Prince was obviously compelled to renounce all his titles and privileges, but by virtue of his birth, he always remained an Archduke. There is no mistaking it: to judge by his features, his presence, and his spirit, Don Justo Armas remained to the day of his death one of the most distinguished members of the House of Habsburg. And it is understood that the House of Habsburg, or House of Austria, was ever the most distinguished in Europe.

It is true that Vienna, with the flourishing of its universities, of its architecture, and of the fine arts in general, had come to be one of the most civilized and advanced cities in Europe. But in El Salvador the Archduke led a tranquil life, free of all passions and intrigues. On leaving his homeland he took with him the substance of Viennese culture, and to this he added the memory of vast Pampas, the grandiose peaks of the Andes, and the valuable experience of riding out every variety of turbulent storms. In San Salvador, in the peace of a solitary life, the Archduke, by meditation, completed the maturation of his spiritual life and his full communion with the Most High.

He Was Not Maximilian

here are many people in El Salvador who can recall having seen Don Justo Armas. He was a gentleman of an august presence, with kindly face and broad, untroubled brow, who always walked barefoot. He was highly literate. He spoke six languages. One gathered from his talk that he was an Austrian who had lived many years in Argentina.

I remember him as of medium height, broad-shouldered, and of a ruddy complexion. He had blue eyes and a gaze at once sweet, caressing, firm, and penetrating. His hair was of a rather darkish red. He wore a beard very like that of his father the emperor Francis Joseph.

And everyone in El Salvador, people of the new generation, kept on asking why he went barefoot. And the story went the rounds of what happened in the Straits of Magellan where he vowed to the Virgin to walk barefoot the rest of his life if she saved him from the tempest's fury.

It was said that Don Justo was a prince. Clearly he was Habsburg. There were those who said that Don Justo was the Emperor Maximilian. The "captain of the firing squad" (so they said) was also a Mason, like Justo Armas, and only pretended to execute him, but let him escape. Yet he was clearly not Maximilian, though he resembled him so much that no one could deny their kinship. Even had he not been shot and had succeeded in escaping from México, as those who invented this story claim, Maximilian would have returned to his own country. In any event, he would not have taken the long way round, from the Gulf of México to El Salvador via the Straits of Magellan. That would be absurd.

Also, when Don Justo arrived in El Salvador in 1898, he looked the forty years of age he indeed was, and not the sixty-six years of his uncle, the Emperor of México. When Don Justo died in 1936, he looked the seventy-eight he was, and not the one-hundred-and-four that would have been Maximilian. Moreover Maximilian, once outside México, and so out of danger, would have no need to keep his identity hid, nor to lead so isolated a life. Nor would he have passed thirty-one years in hiding, with no one hearing from him between his leaving México in 1867, and his supposed arrival in El Salvador in 1898.

The irrefutable fact is that immediately after his execution at Querétaro, the real mortal remains of Maximilian were taken to Austria by Admiral Wilhelm von Tegethoff. The remains were buried in the Habsburg's family crypt in the monastery of the Capuchin friars in 1867, twenty-two years before Don Justo left Vienna and thirty-two years before he arrived in El Salvador. It appears, then, that the rumors identifying Don Justo and Maximilian are completely absurd however you look at them. All that these rumors indicate is that the kinship of Don Justo and Maximilian was widely known.

In view of the great likeness of the two, it was said at various times that Don Justo could have been the illegitimate son of Maximilian. Had that been so, he would have been proud to publish it to the four winds, and would not have kept his identity hushed the whole length of his life. In short, these stories and others of the sort are so absurd that they deserve no refutation.

I Was in on the Secret

When Rudolf, in Austria, was the Archduke, he either wore no beard, or wore sideburns, or just a small, pointed beard. But when he was Justo Armas, in El Salvador, the Archduke always wore a beard very like that of the Emperor Francis Joseph. He must have wanted people to know that he was the Archduke and Crown Prince, but without saying so, for during the tragedy of Mayerling he gave his word to leave his homeland for ever and to conceal his identity. Thanks to that agreement the Archduke was not sequestered, or rather imprisoned in a monastery for the rest of his life, as was Maria Vetsera.

The opinion that Don Justo was Maximilian was apparently

confirmed when at his death, which occurred May 29, 1936, there were found in his desk drawer two small flags arranged in a cross, one Mexican and the other Austrian. But those best informed about Don Justo's identity understood what Don Justo meant by leaving those two small flags in his desk: no more than that he was closely related to the Emperor of México and to the Emperor of Austria. He meant to make the statement that he was the Archduke Rudolf, as my mother had told me shortly before her death on January 17, 1911. In that tragic hour she told me, or rather confirmed what I already knew, that I was the son of Don Justo, and that Don Justo Armas was the Archduke Rudolf. She then recommended that I always greet him with the same respect as I had before. And she gave me advice that I have obeyed all my life to the letter. When my mother died at the age of forty-three, we found ourselves orphans, our father Don Jorge Lardé having died eight years before, in March of 1903, aged forty-four years.

When I was attending grammar school, and later at the National Institute, I always met Don Justo on the way. I would go and he would come along the same side of the street. Always he would greet me very courteously and affectionately. Although we had a mutual understanding, he never told me anything about our kindred, and I respected his prudent silence. Now, with so many years behind me, and with a fuller knowledge of the politics of his homeland and about his family, I understand far better the propriety of his prudence.

I do not think such frequent encounters, on the same sidewalk but in opposite directions, ascribable to accident. Since I was the only member of his family in El Salvador, surely he took much comfort in setting eyes on me. And I felt happy. To remember his strong, sweet, and affectionate gaze, which pierced to the depth of the soul, is alone a treasure to me greater than a million dollars.

When the government of El Salvador became cognizant of Don Justo's identity and of his difficult economic situation, it sought a discreet way to help him. With that in mind, it was decided to hold a series of receptions in the Presidential Palace, and to request Don Justo to organize them. Certainly, those receptions were unnecessary except for the purpose of helping a Prince in distress. And that was how Don Justo got enough money to build up by stages his small business as caterer of parties and banquets. At first my parents, to help him, lent him the table service of the Europa Hotel. After a while Don Justo managed to buy all he needed to make his business a going concern, a business which was sufficient for his needs for the rest of his life.

He Was A Mystery

Don Justo was a mystery. He had few friends. He did not go to parties. People spoke of him as "the barefoot gentleman." And the questions of the curious were asked again and again. "Who is this gentleman? Why does he go barefoot? Who are his parents?" Parents unknown. "Who are his brethren?" Family unknown. "Where did he come from?" Place of origin unknown. "What is he really doing?" A mystery. Catering parties and banquets is not what could fulfill and satisfy one so full of life as was Don Justo. What did Don Justo do to meet the needs of the spirit?

Few know the work done by Archduke Rudolf in Austria, or Don Justo Armas in El Salvador, in relation to the freeing of European society from the trammels of obscurantism which towards the end of the last century still hindered the work of such men of genius as Freud. And in the nineteenth century many ideas from the age of Machiavelli and Loyola still prevailed, with a basic guiding tenet that in both secular and religious politics, one must consider the ends to be achieved without permitting the choice of means to be influenced by prejudices of a moral order. The end of course would always be for the greater glory of God or Empire. Because of the violent changes that, over the centuries, have characterized the course of human development (such as those called forth by the French Revolution), the Archduke was prone to attitudes diametrically opposed to those of the emperor Francis Joseph. The Emporer favored an autocratic government backed by the powers of the Church and the sword. Important to remember is that in those days the Church in Austria was controlled by the Jesuits.

The Archduke Rudolf, sincerely Catholic and devoutly religious (as was traditional with the Habsburgs), did come nevertheless to be known as a freethinker, and did not conceal his anticlericalism. The Habsburgs had to fight a rather long, drawn-out battle to distinguish between the powers of the church and state. The Jesuits, beneficiaries of the deep affection and respect that the Habsburgs held for them, were the parties most affected by the policy of the separation of church and state. They were the most persistent and most skillful among clerics with a propensity to control secular power. And the Jesuits of those days used every means suggested by Loyola and Machiavelli to realize their aims. There is no suspicion that the anticlerical views of the Archduke Rudolf were antireligious, but they were indeed opposed to the propensities to absolute control (including control of temporal power, that characterized the clergy of his times).

Had the Archduke become Emperor, the alliance of church and state would have been broken forever, and the Empire would have consolidated itself upon a foundation of mutual respect and cooperation among the several ethnic groups that composed it. And there would have been complete freedom of conscience.

But in El Salvador Don Justo Armas was very prudent, and very few people came to know his liberal tendencies, his spiritual breadth, and his aversion to the late nineteenth-century Jesuitism.

Because of this ideological antagonism between father and son, the secret police of the Emperor kept a constant watch on everything the Archduke did. No one visited him unobserved. Even his mail was opened. And it is clear that even in El Salvador, the Austrian secret police continued its vigilance, even as it also kept close watch in Europe on all the moves made by the Empress Elizabeth, up to the day of her death...

Why El Salvador And Not Some Other Country

Doubtless Archduke Rudolf, on leaving his home forever to escape imprisonment and death in a monastery, promised to go as far away as possible, to a country where no one would recognize him. He was almost as well known in the other countries of Europe as in his own. In the big cities of Latin America there were many possibilities of running into compatriots who might recognize him, especially in cities facing the Atlantic. El Salvador was on the Pacific, as though turning its back on the Old World.

El Salvador is a small country, and in those days the foreign colony was quite small. Although Salvadorans have always been very Catholic and devoutly religious, in their politics, the liberal ideas of the French philosophers have prevailed. There is separation of church and state, the cemeteries are secular, education is lay, and in those days there were no Jesuits. All this agreed very well with the Archduke's temperament, which was devoutly religious, and at the same time liberal, anticlerical, and above all anti-Jesuit.

To this later was added his need to live in a tropical climate because of his promise to always walk barefoot for the rest of his life.

In brief, Don Justo found the ideal conditions in El Salvador, because it was a civilized country, small, tropical in climate, remote from Europe, and where he could lead a tranquil, solitary life. That was the best cure for the profound grief that the tragedy of Mayerling caused him — when he was compelled to leave his country forever, against all justice and reason, as shall be illustrated further on.

These are the reasons that logic offers us to explain the decision of Don Justo to go to live in El Salvador. But there are always forces prior and superior to all logic which really decide the most important decisions that we make in life. I refer to subconscious forces that connect us to specific persons unknown to us, however far away they might be. They are forces that come from times past and connect us with the immediate future, and even with the distant future. They are forces that we do not always succeed in understanding with perfect clarity. With very good reason it has been said that the subconscious is the realm of the illogical. However that may be, what is important to me is that the Archduke Rudolf arrived in El Salvador, and arrived on time, well on time, before the date I was due to be born in that country.

Why Justo Armas And Not Another Pseudonym?

Clearly Archduke Rudolf saw the necessity to introduce many reforms into the Austro-Hungarian Empire, so that the different nationalities that composed it — Germans, Hungarians, Croats, Serbians, and so forth — might develop their own culture and follow their own destiny within the unity of the Empire. It has often been remarked that the Habsburg Empire was always "a European necessity" because due to it, European civilization prospered and avoided annihilation by the Turks and Russians. Had they not been united by the central government of the Habsburgs, the different small nationalities would have perished defenseless one after another. The Habsburgs knew how to raise bulwarks and maintain them across the centuries for the defense of civilization.

Although for many centuries communal welfare required total centralization, towards the end of the last century it became necessary also to meet the just aspiration of the different nationalities. But the government of His Imperial Majesty, Francis Joseph, had failed to keep in step with the rhythm of changing tendencies in modern times. It had failed to draw the line between the obedience to the central government and the liberty that national minorities needed to accomplish their own destiny within the imperial conglomerate. And the just aspirations of people were repressed by the combined powers of the Church and of arms. For the Emperor, discipline and respect for tradition were essential. And that discipline and tradition had to be maintained at all costs.

Archduke Rudolf understood that times were changing. The ideas of the French philosophers had entered into the normative standards of world public opinion as a result of the French Revolution, and had spread throughout Europe by the conquering armies of Napoleon Bonaparte. With the passage of time, imperial absolutism had become unjust. Adjustments were necessary to answer to the awakening new political standards of national minorities. Something had brought their aspirations to ferment, and those aspirations needed to be understood and given leadership before it was too late. Moreover, the First World War was already in the making, and Archduke Rudolf, being Crown Prince, was obliged to prepare himself for dealing with the situation the moment he ascended the throne. There was not time to lose. It was a pressing reality, and no one could tell how much he had at his disposal before he became Emperor.

In view of all the problems, ever more difficult, that were arising both within and outside the Empire, it was quite possible that the Emperor might decide to abdicate in favor of the heir apparent. But there was no way of knowing when he would do so. The Archduke preferred to bide his time, but the leaders of the national minorities were losing their patience. Meanwhile, the secret police shrewdly kept an eye on the secret plans and thoughts of those leaders. The situation was grave. The leading thought of the Archduke was to insure the defense, progress, and well-being of the Empire as a whole, without neglecting the just aspirations of its constituent nationalities. And the Archduke understood that those aspirations would have to be defended by force of arms.

Taken as a whole, the political ideas of the Crown Prince were diametrically opposed to the ideas of his father the Emperor. The clergy sided with the Emperor. The entire nobility enjoyed the benefits and privileges of the establishment and of course agreed with the Emperor. But the leaders of the different nationalities that made up the Empire were in agreement with the political ideals of the

Archduke. This ideological distance between the Emperor and the Crown Prince was the essential cause of the disaster of Mayerling. During the tragedy, the Crown Prince saw himself compelled to renounce all his privileges of nobility, leave Austria forever, and conceal his true identity under a pseudonym.

The pseudonym he adopted expresses his opinion about the role that the imperial army should always play, namely to support justice with arms, and not to perpetuate injustices with the combined forces of the Church and the sword. He was above all a JUST man, as well as a distinguished military man who knew the force of ARMS. Archduke Rudolf, in truth and with no room for doubts, was Don JUSTO ARMAS. And that pseudonym, in Spanish, with the meaning it has in Spanish, was adopted by the Archduke from the moment he chose to live in exile for the rest of his life. At his request, during the tragedy of Mayerling he was provided with a valid passport for an ordinary citizen, "Herr Justo Armas."

The Jesuit Scandal

Don Justo Armas was a solitary man. At least, after the tragedy of Mayerling, and after the shipwreck in the Straits of Magellan, and after he had received the news of the assassination of his mother, Don Justo, in El Salvador, was a solitary man. But when he was called Rudolf, in Austria, the impetuous, youthful, and attractive Prince was not a solitary man — quite the contrary. He had a very active political, social, and intellectual life. He liked both military science and natural science, but his chief interests were the philosophical views of the free-thinkers. This quickly provoked antagonism among the clergy. At the time in Austria, the clergy was wholly dominated by the Jesuits. Responsibility is ascribed to them for having planned the feigned affair of Rudolf and Maria Vetsera, and turning it into a scandal of major proportions.

The Jesuits have always led a life more military and political than religious and contemplative. They are controversial even within the Church to the extent that in 1773 Pope Clement XIV suppressed this religious order and it ceased to exist for over forty years until 1814, when Pope Pious VII revived it again. The order has been a special problem to many Popes and even to this day Pope John Paul II recently suspended the normal workings of the Jesuits, dismissed their leader and replaced him with two men of his confidence, Paolo Dezza and Joseph Pittau. The problem this time is the well-known political work of the Jesuits in favor of the left.

In Vienna the Jesuits controlled all cultural, political, and religious life in their role as confessors, tutors of the royal family, university professors, and sermonizers. Confessions and confidential insinuating conversations with ladies in high society were their most effective weapons, providing access to every type of inside information in politics. They then would use this information with the intent to blackmail or defame. It is believed that they were the ones who invented and circulated rumors of every possible variety to discredit Archduke Rudolf, whose lofty moral no one who knew him well could question.

They say that Archduke Rudolf was considering a divorce to marry Baroness Maria Vetsera. But that was an impossibility in the Austria of those days. If those amorous adventures of the Archduke had in fact occurred, they could easily have been overlooked, and condoned by a pious comprehension. But in a Viennese society dominated by the Jesuits, the material and political interests of the clergy prevailed, and they saw themselves threatened by the liberal tendencies of the Crown Prince.

Archduke Rudolf was a man of high political and social ideals. He was committed to a program of reform that implied total separation of church and state. And the great scandal that the Jesuits contrived, being set afoot to prevent such a reform, led to the tragedy of Mayerling. The thirtieth of January, 1889, the Austrian government published the frightful news that in the hunting lodge of Mayerling the Archduke and Baroness Maria Vetsera had died in tragic circumstances.

Nothing Is So Secret That It Shall Not Be Manifest

It is generally taken for a fact that Prince Rudolf slew his beloved Baroness Maria Vetsera and afterwards committed suicide. Nevertheless, in many books, and even in brief textbook outlines and encyclopedia articles, one finds that the official version of what happened at Mayerling is open to doubt. It is obvious that there was a secret. The official version is false. If it had been true, there would have been no need to compel all who were in the know to swear not to reveal what really had happened at Mayerling. And it would not have been necessary to withdraw from the state archives of Austria the files of official documents bearing on the life and pretended death of Archduke Rudolf. It would also not have been necessary to compel the family of Maria Vetsera to sign a document falsely declaring that Maria Vetsera had committed suicide. All this secretiveness gave rise to many and extraordinary romances about the pretended death of the Archduke and the Baroness. These romances could not be more ingenious, more absurd, or farther from the truth.

The truth is that Maria Vetsera was put away for the rest of her life in an austere Carmelite monastery. And the truth is that after Mayerling, the Archduke arrived in El Salvador as Justo Armas. Don Justo Armas told my mother Doña Amelie Arthés de Lardé that he, Don Justo, was the Archduke Rudolf. My mother is one of many witnesses in the know about the true identity of Don Justo. And she was a direct witness, for she knew of it straight from the lips of Don Justo. If the Prince told her so, surely it was because he desired that I, his only male child, should also know it at the proper time. And I bear solemn witness to the truth of what I say, namely that she told me, a little before her death, that he, Don Justo, told her that he, Don Justo, was the Archduke Rudolf, Crown Prince and son of the Emperor Francis Joseph.

She kept the secret of Don Justo's identity, as he desired, to the day of her death. I also have kept it, even as she urged me. But now, as I have already said, His Majesty the Emperor Francis Joseph and all of his generation being dead, and dead Don Justo Armas, the truth can hurt no one. I think I can speak now, especially since at my age, over eighty, no one can profit from doing me harm.

Documents Are Not Always Authenticating Evidence

y birth certificate says that I am the legitimate son of Doña Amelie Arthés de Lardé and her husband Don Jorge Lardé. It also says that I was born in San Salvador.

That is not so. Don Jorge Lardé was my father by adoption, but Don Justo was my natural father. And I was born at ten in the morning, June 30, 1899, in the Hacienda Asino, property of my parents, located on the shores of Lake Ilopango, within the jurisdiction of the town of Ilopango. So then, regardless of what my birth certificate says, my natural father was not Don Jorge Lardé, nor was I born in San Salvador. Though it must be taken seriously into consideration, an official document (whatever the government that backs it) cannot always be accepted as sufficient to verify the facts it affirms. This is true whether it be a document from the Austrian government affirming the tragic death of Archduke Rudolf and Baroness Maria Vetsera, or a Salvadoran document, like my birth certificate.

Of course, what someone's birth certificate says about him, whoever he is, does not provide conclusive proof of who his natural father is. Only his mother can know that for sure. The birth certificate is not a definitive proof. What the mother has to say is among the more important considerations. One must also judge by physical likeness or dissimilarity. Does the child resemble the person named as father in the birth certificate? Does he resemble the person generally rumored to be the father? Does he resemble the person that the mother names?

To judge by photographs, when I was thirty I closely resembled Archduke Rudolf at that age. The likeness is as that between twin brothers. The only patent difference is that at that age, I still shaved, while he wore a mustache. At the age I now have, a little over eighty years, I still resemble Don Justo closely, but I resemble more the Emperor Francis Joseph during his last years. Often people who were probably of Austrian origin have stopped me walking along the streets of New York, to tell me that I am the living picture of His Imperial Majesty, Francis Joseph. An elderly lady, who, when a child, was personally acquainted with the Emperor, told me that she thought that the Emperor had risen from the dead when she saw me. Others had already told me as much.

At home we knew quite well who Don Justo was, and it was also known in Salvadoran social circles around the turn of the century. But the secret had to be kept, out of respect for the Archduke's wishes. And I, since childhood, have always been responsible, and have always understood the need to keep the secret. But now, as I have said, I can reveal it.

Two Significant Facts

bout 1960 Archduke Otto and his brother went to El Salvador. Why did they go? I do not know. There was no reason, no apparent motive for their visit. But those who love gossip spread the story that they had come to see whether Don Justo, who died in 1936, had left a fortune to which they, Archduke Otto and his brother, could lay claim. I scarcely think they would have come for that. But their visit to El Salvador, whatever the actual motive may have been, is quite significant.

Shortly after that, the government of El Salvador sent to the Austrian government the official dossier on the arrival in El Salvador of Archduke Rudolf, known under the name of Justo Armas, and his residence in that country to the day of his death. And with that, the government of El Salvador closed that chapter in its relations with the government of Austria.

This fact, the turning over of the dossier on Don Justo to the Austrian government, is quite significant. His Majesty's government, as we know, removed from the state archives of Austria everything bearing on the alleged death of Archduke Rudolf. That weeding out culminated in the turning over of the official Salvadoran dossier on Justo Armas. The decision and orders of Emperor Francis Joseph were backed by irrevocable authority. Even after his death his policy and determination remained firm: to wipe out of the minds of his contemporaries all memory of his son, so that not the slightest trace might remain of his continued existence after his alleged death at Mayerling.

But now, in view of all that is disclosed in this memoir, no one need feel obliged to keep the secret.

Everyone Suffered

on Justo was a solitary man. His father, Emperor Francis Joseph (with his son and wife both lost) was likewise a solitary man. Both father and son must have suffered on account of the tragedy of Mayerling and its distant effect, the Jesuitical and Machiavellian assassination of the Empress Elizabeth. The Emperor must have suffered on taking a decision so contrary to the sentiments of a father, merely to comply with the duties of the crown. These were duties that were badly misunderstood because of the pressure that the Jesuits applied within the alliance of Church and State. The son must have suffered to the depth of his heart when faced with the hardness of his father and the lack of understanding of persons of influence within the government. And he must have suffered much from the obligation to part forever from his father and mother, his wife Stephanie, his daughter Elizabeth, all his childhood friends, his personal belongings, and his homeland, of which he would later have become Emperor if the catastrophe of Mayerling had never occurred.

What became of Baroness Maria Vetsera? How many days, or months, or years did she survive in the convent where she was imprisoned among nuns, a convent that was truly her tomb? How did they treat her? Did she find consolation in meditation? And the Empress Elizabeth, mother of Archduke Rudolf, must have suffered unspeakably. Only mothers could understand all the pain, confusion, and desperation of that woman on hearing it said that her son had committed suicide at Mayerling. She could no longer remain in Vienna, where everything that she came across reminded her of her son.

There is no doubt that the Emperor, who could count upon a powerful and well organized secret police, kept himself informed about the activities and plans of Her Majesty, the Empress Elizabeth, as well as about the activities of his son and the stages of his long journey to his country of destination. After January 29, 1889, when her son disappeared from Austria, the Empress travelled constantly from country to country in Europe, to forget, to forget... Or perhaps to seek out... What is certain is that when Vienna received the notice that her son went barefoot in distant lands, and would soon arrive at his destination, the Empress died in tragic circumstances. She was assassinated on the shores of Lake Geneve, September 10, 1898, at the age of sixty-one.

The Secret At All Costs

It was requisite to keep the secret of all that had in fact happened at Mayerling, and it was hard for a mother to keep silent. The Empress had voyaged incessantly as though in search of her son because of some premonitions that he was not dead, and that she might find him. And she would have gone to the remotest land, had it been necessary, to see him again and be with him for the rest of her life. In such a case the secret would have been made public and the house of Habsburg dishonored. It was requisite to keep the secret *at all cost*. In any event, the Empress was assassinated the same year that the Austrian Consul in El Salvador informed the government of Francis Joseph that Archduke Rudolf had arrived and went about the streets of San Salvador barefoot. The official report of the Austrian government that same year, 1898, was that the Empress died assassinated by the anarchist Luigi Luchemi. But can we believe the official reports bearing on all this tragedy? The hand of Luchemi may have performed the act, but who was responsible? Who planned it or allowed it?

Of course it is known that she died assassinated. The problem is to clear up how she could have been assassinated when her comings and goings were always attended by a detachment of the Emperor's secret police, solely to protect her. The problem is to figure out whether it was a political assassination, that is, a distant consequence of the tragedy of Mayerling. For someone fully informed about all the circumstances of the tragedy of Mayerling, no other view is possible. And if it was a political assassination, who were those who plotted it and who authorized it? I do not even want to think of that.

I do not want to think of the profound suffering of Don Justo Armas. I do not want to think of all that had crossed his mind when, not long after he arrived at his destination, El Salvador, he received notice that his mother had been assassinated on the shores of Lake Geneve.

What a tragedy of tragedies!

Why do these things happen!

Why?

II. The Two Archdukes

They Were Up To Something

*A*rchduke Rudolf and his cousin Johann Salvator, son of Maria Antonia, Grand Duchess of Tuscany, were about the same age. In 1889, when the tragedy of Mayerling occurred, Rudolf was 31 and Johann Salvator, 36. The lives of the two archdukes had run parallel. The two shared liberal and anticlerical ideas. Both reflected on the need to introduce drastic reforms into the Empire before it was too late. Both saw how serious the internal difficulties of the Empire had become, and how serious the political movements in ferment throughout Europe were, movements that later led to World War One.

Both wanted the Austrian Empire to make effective preparations to face the coming storm. Both understood that, however one looked at it, a break with the past was urgent if the Empire and the prestige of the House of Austria were to be saved.

Such a topic could not be broached with His Imperial Majesty, Francis Joseph, because of his strongly conservative tendencies, and because he believed in the alliance of church and state. There was no way of bringing up the topic of how urgently the Empire needed to change its course; he was intransigent and autocratic through and through. But Rudolf, being Crown Prince, had to keep himself ready for any emergency. There was no way of telling in how many years he would have to assume the throne. He had to plan forthwith a transformation of the Empire. Rudolf discussed all his plans with his cousin, Johann Salvator.

The two Archdukes did not find it easy to exchange their views because both were under constant surveillance by the secret police of the Emperor, and their correspondence was opened and read. This is why they wrote each other in a private cipher and sent their letters by messengers in whom they could place implicit trust. Clearly, the two Archdukes were planning how to save the Empire from certain catastrophe if a war should break out with Russia, and the other European powers intervened.

They understood clearly that the world war would break out in a few years, and that if the thorough and drastic reforms that they were making plans for were not introduced in time, the Empire would be dismembered and the House of Austria could lose the preponderant position that it had maintained for so many centuries in European politics. Despite their secrecy and all the precautions that they took, the Emperor knew that the two Archdukes were planning something behind his back. He knew Archduke Rudolf was planning something for a distant future. But he also knew that progressive elements in the Empire wanted to force the pace of events to make changes in the immediate future, even without the approval of the Crown Prince.

The Critical Moment

L ate in January 1889 there appeared in Vienna the news that in the hunting lodge of Mayerling had been found the bodies of Archduke Rudolf and Baroness Maria Vetsera. But this was not so. The Baroness was closed up in a convent, and the Archduke made ready to leave Austria forever. After he adopted the pseudonym "Justo Armas," it is quite possible that the Archduke disguised himself and stayed awhile in hiding in Birstein, as a guest of Johann Salvator's sister, Luisa Princess Icenburg, or some other place in Germany, before moving on.

Archduke Rudolf found himself compelled to renounce his titles of nobility, take the pseudonym "Justo Armas," and leave his homeland forever. Archduke Johann Salvator similarly decided to renounce his privileges, take "Johann Orth" as a pseudonym, buy a merchant vessel, study to become its captain, and take up maritime trade. In brief, he decided to leave his homeland forever. Immediately after the tragedy of Mayerling, he began his studies to receive the title of captain in the merchant marine. He graduated before the year was over. Soon afterwards he bought in Hamburg a merchant ship, the Saint Margaret.

Johann Orth had enough experience to captain a ship in Mediterranean waters, but he had never crossed the Atlantic. Having bought the ship, he hired a crew of sailors that he trusted and personally took the ship to Chatham. In this English port he hired three officers and a captain. He decided to make the Atlantic crossing as second-in-command. In England, he was able to find a contract to ship a cargo of cement from Chatham to La Plata, Argentina, and another to ship back a cargo of saltpeter from Valparaíso, Chile, on his return trip to England.

From England To The Straits Of Magellan

A fter some difficulties, Johann Orth left Chatham for South America on March 16, 1890, and eleven weeks later arrived at La Plata, where he delivered the cement. In La Plata, Johann Orth discharged the captain and two officers. He likewise discharged a couple of sailors whom he could no longer trust. He himself took over as captain of the Saint Margaret. We do not know whether either of the discharged sailors was a member of the Imperial secret police. That police was effective and sufficiently well-organized so as to have been able to infiltrate the crew of the ship.

Despite his inexperience, Johann Orth decided to continue on towards Valparaíso. He left La Plata for Cape Horn on July 12, that is, at the worse season for crossing to the Pacific. Violent storms were blowing at freezing temperatures. The Saint Margaret was sighted, July 31st, near Cape Horn, defying the stormy seas. In view of the fury of the tempest, he decided, very much against his will, to turn back a ways in search of a less perilous route. But he lacked experience to deal with such seas, and the ship finally went down in the Straits of Magellan.

When news of the shipwreck reached Europe, Emperor Francis Joseph ordered a search for the vessel, but no trace was found either of the Saint Margaret, or of the men aboard. The Emperor knew who was on the crew because the secret police informed him. And it would have been only natural for His Majesty to be deeply concerned for the safety of *one* of the crew members of the Saint Margaret.

For many years, rumors circulated that Archduke Johann Salvator had survived the shipwreck, and that he had been seen in remote regions of Argentina. No one could believe that so young a man, and so vigorous, could have perished. Twenty-one years later, in 1911, the Austrian authorities finally accepted for fact the death of Archduke Johann Salvator.

The last Habsburg Emperor, however, did not hesitate to confirm ten years later that Johann Orth was not dead but living in South America. There is no doubt that His Highness Charles I knew one of the Archdukes had survived the shipwreck in the Straits of Magellan, and he knew that the distinguished person several travelers had seen was not Johann Salvator but rather the other Archduke, who lived a few years in Argentina. He knew also that this person was no longer in South America, but in Central America. Charles knew very well of whom he spoke.

The Other Archduke

eyond question, Archduke Rudolf, having adopted the pseudonym of Justo Armas, arrived in El Salvador in September 1898, where he lived until the day of his death, May 29, 1936, being seventy-eight years of age. Archduke Rudolf and his cousin, Archduke Johann Salvator shared the same temperament and the same ideals. They pursued the same political objectives, and together they were planning, in secret, their future activities. Together they decided what they would do in the event of discovery.

After he took the pseudonym of Justo Armas, the Archduke doubtless disguised himself and went into hiding somewhere in Germany while Archduke Johann Salvator took his degree as captain and bought a ship to take up maritime trade. The Saint Margaret left Chatham, reached La Plata, and sank in the Straits of Magellan. And Archduke Rudolf, alias Justo Armas, traveled from Europe to El Salvador via a ship that sank in the Straits of Magellan. That ship must have been the Saint Margaret.

This inevitable conclusion having been accepted requires that, in conformity with previously agreed plans, Archduke Rudolf disguised as a simple sailor, took ship on the Saint Margaret at a German port, probably Hamburg, and disappeared into the rest of the crew. As the ship left Europe ever farther behind, the Archduke felt less keenly the need to totally conceal his identity. From then on he was a particular friend of the captain. The violent emotional storm of Mayerling was a thing of the past. He felt relaxed. But the tranquility began to fade away as another storm appeared on the horizon. This time it was a matter of a storm with freezing winds and towering waves. The Virgin had already performed a miracle and Don Justo proved once again that by strength of faith the most terrifying situations can be faced down.

We know that Archduke Rudolf, after crossing the Pampas of Argentina and after having led the life of a rancher for many years, his spiritual strength made immense by such sufferings and all the difficulties he had to overcome, arrived at last in his country of destination, El Salvador, in September 1898. His arrival in El Salvador was his salvation. There he met Don Jorge Lardé and his wife Doña Amelie Arthés de Lardé, who helped him to establish his small business as a caterer for parties and banquets. There he met my godfather, the young lieutenant in the French Army, who later became the distinguished General Henri Giraud. There he met my godmother, Doña Adriana Cabrolier Arthés, the Bellegarrigue family, the Arbizú Bosques, the Arrieta Rossis, and other people who could understand him. There, in San Salvador, he led a peaceful life for as long as he lived.

In Austria remained the pomp of Empire, the pageantry, the haughtiness, and ostentation. In Austria remained the outward show, which is all that the base multitude can see and understand. In El Salvador lived the true Archduke. The noble spirit whose great energy was put to the proof by the violence of passions and of tempests. The man, the true Rudolf von Habsburg, Archduke by birth, whose high morality no one who knew him well could question, lived a peaceful and deeply pious life in El Salvador to the day of his death.

The Year 1860

The Crown Prince was born with a delicate constitution, as if born prematurely, but with extraordinary spirit. By God's Grace he was born to be, as his father was, Emperor of Austria, Apostolic King of Hungary, King of Jerusalem, King of Bohemia, King of Dalmatia, King of Transylvania, etc., etc. He never achieved that destiny due to the intrigues and confabulations of the Jesuit clergy and the ultra-conservatives led by Ministers Taaffe and Kalnoky.

When Rudolf was born on August 21, 1858, his father, the Emperor Francis Joseph, immediately named him Colonel-in-Chief of the Imperial and Royal 19th Infantry Regiment and placed in his cradle the Order of the Golden Fleece. Moved by a desire to have his son become the most distinguished monarch in history, the Emperor had him separated from his mother, Empress Elizabeth, from 1860 on. This was done in order to place him under tutors who would endow him with an extensive scientific, political, philosophical, and military culture, and who would also inculcate a strong sense of discipline that would give him the stamina to confront and overcome challenging situations.

One of his first tutors, Count Leopold Gondrecourt, was a rude, cruel, and brutal man. To educate the young prince he would make use of incredibly atrocious procedures. For example, when Rudolf was only six years old, he would shoot fire-arms next to his bed at midnight to wake him up. The purpose was to develop in him an alert but calm spirit, foreseeing the possibility that the Prince should have to confront an unexpected uprising during his adolescence. At other times he would shut him in a cage at the zoo and would terrorize him, telling him that the beasts would come to devour him and he would have to defend himself alone. He would be abandoned in the cage for a while.

When the Empress became aware of what was going on, she intervened vigorously in order to have such inhuman tutors changed, before the harm caused the young Prince became irreversible. The new instructors were more human, such as the patient and understanding Count Joseph Latour. The young Archduke was deeply interested in chemistry, especially organic chemistry, bacteriology, the practical uses of electricity, natural sciences, and science in general. Later he became deeply interested in political science, philosophy, and in a very special way, the French philosophers.

A result of his studies were numerous essays. One of these was the very interesting and well know book, *Fifteen Days on the Danube*, for which the University of Vienna conferred upon him an Honorary Doctoral degree. Later he edited the monumental work, *The Austro-Hungarian Monarchy in Words and Pictures*.

In addition to military activities, the Crown Prince participated in various diplomatic missions and he was always praised for his great cultural attainments. Queen Victoria of England considered Archduke Rudolf to be extremely impressive and imposing — to such an extent that a small gossip went around for a while that the Queen was in love with Crown Prince Rudolf.

All these memories remained with the Archduke throughout his life. Pleasant memories, memories of exact sciences learned, and memories of hopes and ambitions which were part of him at one time. But a persistent and important date remained fixed in his memory, the haunting memory of the year 1860, when he lost the company of his mother the Empress and was put in the charge of his tutors, one of whom was extremely brutal and cruel. This date, 1860, when at the age of two he was separated from his mother, was ever present in his memory. This date would come back to his consciousness: 1860... 1860... 1860...

And he would ask without finding any answer, and always more indignant: Why was I left without my mother? Why? WHY?

III. Mayerling

The Trap

𝕬 t home we always knew that no one died during the tragedy of Mayerling, neither Baroness Maria Vetsera nor Archduke Rudolf. The decision had been made to put both away in monastic seclusion for the rest of their lives, and then announce the false news that both died tragically. The Archduke rebelled against this, and finally it was agreed that he would adopt a pseudonym to hide his identity and would leave Austria forever — to settle in a distant land where no one would recognize him. Only the Baroness would be locked up in a convent for the rest of her life. This was one of the things that Archduke Rudolf told my mother when he came to El Salvador. So for me it is the truth. And whatever information the Archduke provided my mother is the light that has guided my investigations. Many contradictory, absurd, and even calumnious things have been said, but with that light the truth can be found out, as will appear in the sequel.

Liberal and progressive elements felt that the best answer to the many and hard problems that were arising within and without the Empire would be for the Emperor to abdicate in favor of the Crown Prince. It seemed clear that Archduke Rudolf was better able than his father to set the Empire on a new course that might meet the new needs of the time. But the Archduke was strongly opposed to compelling the Emperor to abdicate. Moreover, the leadership of the Empire, being quite conservative, feared that their liberal opponents might make overly-radical decisions. To insure against anyone thinking of forcing the Emperor to abdicate, they decided to eliminate Archduke Rudolf, who was the hope of the liberals. And for that purpose they thought it best, after long discussions, to put him away in a convent for the rest of his life, and declare that he committed suicide.

As usually happens in a conflict between liberal and conservative forces, the ecclesiastical authorities fell in with the conservatives and helped plan the seclusion of the Archduke in a monastery. Count Taaffe, Minister of the Interior, Count Kalnoky, Minister of Foreign Affairs, Count Hoyos, Privy Councillor of the Emperor, and Prince Philip of Coburg, brother in law of Archduke Rudolf, met to work out the details of the plan.

The discussion got under way. Secluding someone in a monastery is easily arranged with the Apostolic Nuncio. It is in the Church's interest to prevent Archduke Rudolf from becoming

Emperor. Then someone suggests that nothing could better account for a suicide than an impossible love affair. An impossible affair? The Archduke is a man of excellent morals, devoted to his family, dedicated to his studies and the Empire's problems. He has neither the time nor the least inclination to complicate his life with adventures of the heart. An impossible entanglement... But how! In the Archduke's case, that is absurd.

Someone suggests that perhaps one could make use of Baroness Maria Vetsera. Everyone knows that the Baroness is profoundly interested in the Prince. Whenever they saw each other her gaze followed him as though to devour him with her eyes. But the Archduke showed not the least interest in the Baroness.

In such a case perhaps one could find a third person to help smooth over the difficulty. But who would that be? None other than Countess Larisch. She is a friend of the Baroness Vetsera and a close friend of the Archduke, besides being his cousin. In addition, she often finds herself in economic straits. The important thing was to have at least the appearance that the Baroness had become his mistress.

A few days later Countess Larisch got things under way and in mid January 1889 it seemed as if Maria Vetsera had met the Archduke Rudolf. And the slanders that she was already his mistress were spread about in preparation for the projected tragedy. It was probably Prince Philip of Coburg who took on the responsibility of informing Archduke Rudolf of what had been decided on. The excellent and formidable secret police of Count Taaffe knew everything. The decision arrived at was intended to avoid any political scandal by substituting the fiction of a tragedy resulting from an impossible love affair. The two of them, the Archduke and the Baroness, would be put away for life in suitable monasteries, and everyone would act out the sham of their having died tragically. But the Archduke would have nothing to do with such a scheme, agreeing instead to perpetual exile. And he began making his preparations for departure. He had but a few days at his disposal and much to do in them. Count Kalnoky, Minister of Foreign Affairs, assumed responsibility for providing him with a valid Austrian passport for an ordinary citizen, "Herr Justo Armas."

The Last Farewells

On January 27, everyone in Vienna was at a party thrown by the German Ambassador to celebrate the birthday of Kaiser Wilhelm II. Ministers of state, high government officials, distinguished representatives of the arts and sciences, members of the nobility, including Baroness Helena Vetsera and her daughter Maria, were invited to the reception. Archduke Rudolf and his wife Stephanie arrived shortly before his father the Emperor. When Emperor Francis Joseph arrived, Archduke Rudolf pressed the hand extended to him, and bowed most reverently, showing the utmost respect for His Majesty. This pressing of hands was their parting gesture, their last farewells, when father and son saw each other for the last time.

That night the Archduke spoke with Kalnoky and Hoyos about the "hunt" he was to go on that coming Tuesday and Wednesday, January 29 and 30, at Mayerling. He requested Count Hoyos to discuss the matter with Prince Philip of Coburg to remind him to arrive Tuesday 29 at Mayerling in time for breakfast. And at that he left for Mayerling.

Rudolf had ready a telegram addressed to his wife Stephanie, asking her to present his excuses to his father for being unable to attend a family dinner that the Emperor was giving the evening of Tuesday 29; he had caught a bad cold on the road. The Archduke gave orders that once the telegram was sent no one was to remain on duty at the telegraph office at Mayerling, and so severed all communication with the outside world for the rest of the day. The telegram arrived one hour before dinner was to begin.

After breakfast, after orders had been given about sending the telegram and possibly a few letters of farewell, the Archduke took leave of Hoyos and Coburg, and got ready to leave Mayerling for the frontier. That day, Tuesday January 29, Maria Vetsera would have gone in the morning to the lodge of Mayerling to see the Archduke. Instead of driving to Mayerling, as she had expected, the carriage took her to the convent of nuns, that isolated her completely from the world for the remainder of her life.

Immediately after the tragedy, the Emperor Francis Joseph gave orders that the strict order of Carmelites be installed in the Lodge of Mayerling. How many days, or how many months, or how many years did the Baroness survive the rigorous monastic life for which she had not the least vocation?

Once Maria Vetsera had been taken to the convent, the coachman Bratfisch drove to Mayerling to take the Archduke and his servant Loschek to the railway station. Loschek went with the Archduke by train as far as the frontier, then sent a coded telegram to Prince Philip of Coburg, who had returned to Vienna, reporting that the Archduke had crossed the frontier.

The Farce

he next morning, Wednesday January 30, Prince Philip of Coburg returned to Mayerling. Loschek was already back from the frontier. The three of them met — Hoyos, Coburg, and Loschek — and the talks got down to contriving the details of the plot.

First they decided that Rudolf and Maria Vetsera had been discovered dead that morning. A pool of blood lay on the floor beside Rudolf. Probably they poisoned themselves with potassium cyanide, for that causes hemorrhages. That was the first report to reach Vienna. Then they found out that cyanide does not cause hemorrhages, so they created another story. In the afternoon Vienna was informed that Archduke Rudolf died of apoplexy.

The coffin with Rudolf's remains arrived at the Imperial Palace in the early hours of the morning on January 31. It now turned out that the Archduke had died of a heart attack. Soon afterwards, it appeared that he had not had a heart attack after all. The doctor who had examined the cadavers, judging by the position of the revolver beside the right hand of the Archduke, and by the bullet wounds also, had come to the conclusion that the Archduke killed the Baroness, and then shot himself.

The Burials

he next problem was to have a burial with the blessing of the Church. Canon law permits the Church to give its blessing in case of suicide only when the deceased took his life at a time when he was deranged. So one needed to hold an autopsy and have the doctor certify that here was a case of mental derangement.

On February 1, the document was ready, and it was signed by the doctor who lent himself to the farce. The autopsy proved that the Archduke killed himself with a bullet in the skull. Moreover, examination had revealed certain malformations in the structure of the skull which might be conducive to abnormal mental conditions.

With this, public opinion was satisfied and the clergy agreed to a burial with all the ceremony of the Church. The coffin bearing the supposed mortal remains of the Archduke was placed in the Habsburg family crypt at the church of the Capuchin Friars. The Emperor Francis Joseph preserved his serenity during the whole ceremony, but at the end, when the coffin was lowered into the crypt, he could no longer control himself, and began to weep profusely. To be exact, he wept profusely for his son's loss not to the grave but to exile.

The members of the Court of Inquiry, who went to Mayerling to investigate the circumstances of the Prince's death, were bound by oath to keep all the facts secret. What they would have to say thereafter is that the Archduke slew the Baroness and then committed suicide. As for the supposed corpse of the Baroness, they let out that it had been buried in a neighboring cemetery, in conditions of utmost secrecy. The head of the local civil administration was told to make the necessary entries in the official records, and to ensure that they tallied with the official version of the death. The family of Maria Vetsera was made to sign a document falsely declaring that she had committed suicide.

Calumnies

*A*fter the first tergiversations about the death of Rudolf and Maria Vetsera, it became necessary to continue inventing new lies and calumnies, and add confusion to confusion. It was known that Rudolf could not possibly have committed suicide, much less because of an impossible love affair, and even less because in love with Maria Vetsera. Everyone knew that he had not the least interest in that fatuous and flirtatious Baroness.

To confuse the situation further, Hoyos and his collaborators made up a story that Rudolf wanted to get a divorce to marry Maria

Vetsera. They suggested that he had shown suicidal tendencies before, and that she had shown her determination to die. They forged letters and all that was needed to back up their fictions. And there was no lack of people who enjoyed spreading any calumny they could. To complete the farce, all documents that might shed light on the realities of Rudolf's honorable life or the realities of what happened at Mayerling were destroyed by Taaffe's orders or by order of the Emperor.

Falsehoods and calumnies continue to be invented and repeated along the same lines. What is generally accepted as though it were true is the official version that claims that Prince Rudolf slew his mistress, Baroness Maria Vetsera, and then committed suicide. But in many books and almost all encyclopedias which mention the subject, one finds that many doubts surround the official version of what happened at Mayerling. There obviously was a secret, but there is no secret that shall not come abroad. The truth always wins out.

He Arrived On Time

Before he left Austria, the Archduke adopted the pseudonym "Justo Armas" and he gave his word to keep his identity secret for the rest of his life. And he kept the secret as close as his heart allowed. But the moment arrived when, for reasons easy to understand, he revealed the secret to my mother Doña Amelie Arthés de Lardé. She, upon dying, trusted the secret to me and asked me never to reveal it. She did not enter much into details because little time remained. A few hours later she departed.

All my life I have felt under restraint in dealing with this whole subject. But at last I have decided to shed light on the truth of all that happened to the Archduke, not only for my own personal health and peace of mind, but also and above all, to pay his due to a great man, a person of great intellectual endowment, heir of great traditions, and of a morality too lofty for anyone who knew him well to cast doubts.

To repeat, essentially Don Justo Armas was a JUST man. For reasons that cannot be understood with perfect clarity, the Archduke left his fatherland, bound specifically for El Salvador, driven perhaps by a primitive subconscious intuition towards the geographical center of the Western Hemisphere. His journey took time because of the shipwreck in the Straits of Magellan, but finally he arrived in the country of his destination, quite on time before the date I was due to be born at the shores of Lake Ilopango.

IV. The Salvadoran World

The First Friends

We said that the Archduke finally arrived in El Salvador and found lodgings in the Europa Hotel, which in those days was the only hotel in El Salvador. That is how Archduke Rudolf, alias "Justo Armas," met the Lardés, and through them gained entry into Salvadoran society. Archduke Rudolf was cordially received in the Lardé household both because one immediately sensed what sort of man that recently-arrived stranger was, and because of the moral and cultural soundness of the family. And Doña Amelie, being the granddaughter of a French duke, soon understood perfectly the Archduke's delicate situation. Let us remember that the Bourbons were related to the Habsburgs.

The Lardé household, all things considered, and the circle of its friends (which we will describe later on), was the best adapted to help the Archduke adjust to his new life, far from the homeland. That was how Don Justo met Presidente General Rafael Antonio Gutiérrez and General Tomás Regalado, Doctor Reyes Arrieta Rossi, the future Archbishop Monsignor José Alfonso Belloso y Sánchez, the future President Doctor Manuel Enrique Araujo, Don Anselmo Bellegarrigue Bailly, Don Juan Balette, the Arbizú Bosque family, and other members of Salvadoran society. The Archduke also met through the Lardé family the members of the French mission of military advisers that included the future Colonel Julio Bias and General Henri Honoré Giraud.

As we said before, Salvadoran society quickly learned the true identity of Don Justo Armas through the involuntary indiscretion of the employees of the Austrian Consulate. Don Justo Armas personally revealed his identity only to my mother Doña Amelie Arthés de Lardé, who pledged never to disclose it to anyone else.

He Escaped In A Wine Tun

Now, let us recount the background of the Lardé family. During the French Revolution, M. Eloi Martin Lardé, land-owner, grape-grower, and wine merchant, lived in Champagne, to the East of Paris. One day, when wine barrels destined for Louisiana were being loaded on the Marne, he learned that he was on the list of those eminent citizens in the region which the mob then in power had destined for the guillotine the next day. The danger being imminent, he decided to escape within a wine tun unobserved.

The cargo vessel proceeded down the Marne and then the Seine to Rouen. There the cargo was transferred to an ocean-going ship. Once on the high seas, M. Elois Martin got out of the barrel and joined the other passengers, who probably included his wife Mme. Serafine Auberle de Lardé and other kindred. Once he had set up in Baton Rouge, La., the rest of his family followed.

His son M. Louis Florentin Lardé Auberle (Nov. 5, 1816-1879) married Mlle. Maria Agustina Rosette Bourdon Petre (1830–Jan. 25, 1900), daughter of M. Jean Baptiste Bourdon and Rosalie Petre de Bourdon. They had a daughter, Mlle. Marie Coralie Lardé Bourdon (March 3, 1859-1903).

Later, in the wake of the war between the States, Don Florentin, his wife Maria Agustina, and his son Don Jorge (George) moved to Guatemala, where they lived a few years running a farm. Finally, in 1869, they moved to San Salvador and founded the Europa Hotel, and set up house in an apartment next to the hotel. They were also owners of the Hacienda Asino. There they took up farming, ranching, cheese-making, and lime-quarrying.

It Was Best That He Should Marry

When Don Jorge, a rather cultured and refined gentleman, came of age to marry, he had no inclination to marriage or love affairs. He did not feel the least desire for sexual relations. Besides, his constitution was very delicate, and he was prone to pulmonary infections. All he was interested in was his excellent library.

Don Florentin had died towards the end of 1879, and only two family members survived, Doña Agustina, fifty, and Don Jorge, thirty-two. In view of all this, Doña Agustina, afraid that her son might remain bereaved and a bachelor, decided it was best that he should marry. She hunted around in town for a young lady who would do as wife for her son, and found one in Señorita Amelie Arthés Etcheverrie. In those days she was the schoolmistress in sole charge of the parochial school in the village of San Jacinto, now a district of San Salvador. So Doña Agustina invited her to visit regularly, and gave her and her son, Don Jorge, every opportunity to meet in private.

Therefore when Señorita Amelie became pregnant, honor required that Don Jorge marry her. As Doña Maria Agustina had planned, Don Jorge married. The marriage took place on March 23, 1891, when Don Jorge was 32, and Doña Amelie 23. Six months later, September 21 of the same year, their first son was born, my elder brother Don Jorge, father of Don Jorge Lardé y Larín. In a little more than a year, December 21, 1892, was born my elder sister, Señorita Coralie, who died when twenty-four. Later, April 17, 1894, Don Luis was born; he became a dentist and a mathematics professor.

Don Luis was the last bodily son of Don Jorge Lardé Bourdon, for his health was delicate. Neither he nor his family knew what precisely caused him to be so frail. I suspect that he might already have been suffering from the tuberculosis that a few years later carried him off. According to what my mother told me, that illness was not diagnosed until some two or three months before his death.

To Have Children Is Better Than To Have Kittens

Both Don Jorge and Doña Amelie wanted more children. They, like Empress Maria Theresia and her husband Francis Stephen, had strong maternal and paternal feelings. But in the case of my parents, there was the problem of Don Jorge's fragile health. So they agreed by mutual consent that she would be free to continue conceiving children, and that he would adopt them as his own. Doña Agustina, mother of Don Jorge, approved of that arrangement. This solution was unconventional, but theirs, all circumstances taken into consideration, was an unusual problem, and most certainly this solution was compatible with their high moral standards.

Thanks to what Don Jorge and Doña Amelie decided, the Lardé brothers were born and bred there, to contribute richly to the growth of Salvadoran culture, as teachers, writers, artists, and by research in the sciences and philosophy. The heads of the Lardé-Arthés family felt their decision preferable to artificial insemination, the solution that is recommended in such cases to those who seek out the Sanctuary of Lourdes for a miracle. Those who go to Lourdes, of course, return saying that the Virgin did the miracle. And the children never will know who their real father was.

Another solution is to keep cats as pets, as an industrialist and his wife decided, two Salvadoran friends of mine. She could have had children, but he was sterile although not impotent. When but recently wed, and at the wife's insistence, they decided to go to Lourdes and seek a miracle. But on arrival, and to secure his consent, they informed the husband through what curious ways the Virgin works her wonders to perform. He would agree to no such thing, and the couple returned to El Salvador — she disconsolate, and he proud of his manly decision.

She always lamented having never had children of her womb. She might at least have felt happier adopting the children of strangers instead of spending her life fussing over cats. But her husband never put up with the idea of adopting someone else's children. He felt that that would be an insult to his self-dignity.

Doña Adriana Cabrolier Arthés

And, to the point, I remember that my maiden godmother, Doña Adriana Cabrolier Arthés, once told me, "Had I known how sad it is to reach my age and to have had not one child, I assure you that I would have had children BY WHATEVER MEANS POSSIBLE."

It is not a matter of libidinousness but one of strong maternal instincts, as the rectitude of her conduct shows, and her always taking affectionate interest in the neighborhood children. She narrated stories to them and gave them toys and even sewed dresses for the poorest.

I will never forget the look on her face when that so pious and so honorable a spinster told me with a tone of deep and sorrowful conviction, "I would have had children BY WHATEVER MEANS POSSIBLE." She continued a long while gazing as though at a distant horizon, as though thinking of some future opportunity. One could guess her thought and determination, "Once I come to be born again...."

Libidinousness is quite different from strong maternal or paternal feelings. The Habsburg family, for example, was always prolific but never sexually indulgent. The best-known case is that of the Empress Maria Theresia who had sixteen children, and her children Leopold and Maria Carolina who had sixteen and eighteen respectively. The Empress Maria Theresia, besides carrying out her wonderful political work, still found time to be a model wife and loving mother and bring sixteen children into the world. Referring to her children, she once wrote that "One cannot have enough of them. In this matter I am insatiable." You see, the Empress, as my mother Doña Amelie, was a model wife and loving mother; and, as my mother, she had strong maternal feelings.

In this question of whether or not to have children each case is different. Some married couples, though able to have children, prefer not to, and think that that would complicate matters. Others, unable to have any, adopt orphans or foundlings. Whatever solution is adopted, the main point is that it should be based on mutual consent. Any deception, any disloyalty on the part of either of the couple is a form of adultery and must be avoided at all costs.

Our behavior is strongly influenced by our biological heritage, by the psychological influence of family traditions and by the different social contexts in which our careers unfold. All this goes without saying. But there are also forces prior to and higher than these which reason does not always clearly understand.

Now, Doña Adriana Cabrolier Arthés, my godmother, had been engaged once to my godfather, Lieutenant Henri Honoré Giraud. But my aunt Doña Gabriela Arthés de Cabrolier, mother of my godmother, opposed the marriage because, so she said, she did not want any of her younger daughters to marry before her eldest, Doña Maria Luisa. When my godfather, Henri Honoré Giraud, took to return to France, my aunt Doña Gabriela took the engagement ring he had given Doña Adriana from her finger and threw it from the wharf into the sea. My four cousins Doña Maria Luisa, Doña Adriana, Doña Berta, and Doña Rosa, all daughters of my aunt Doña Gabriela, died old and spinsters.

The Lardé, Arthés, Bourdon, And Etcheverrie Families

efore I discuss my brothers in the Lardé Arthés family, I want to record a little about the families of Doña Maria Agustina Rosette Bourdon and Doña Magdalena Etcheverrie, mothers of Don Jorge Lardé Bourdon and of his wife Doña Amelie Arthés Etcheverrie, respectively.

Doña Maria Agustina Rosette Bourdon de Lardé, wife of Don Florentin Lardé and mother of Don Jorge Lardé Bourdon, belonged to a prominent French family, various of whose members distinguished themselves in the fields of mathematics, physics, medicine, and art. One of her uncles, Pierre Louis Marie Bourdon (1779-1854), was professor of mathematics in various universities in France. I remember in the library that we inherited from our father Don Jorge Lardé Bourdon, there was an algebra textbook written by his uncle, the mathematics professor. It must have been *Eléments d'Algèbre* (1843), since he is remembered for this and two other volumes, *Eléments d'Aritmétique* (1821, 21 editions) and *Aplications de l'Algèbre a la Géometrie* (1824).

Those texts, like almost the entirety of the library, were destroyed during the earthquake that began with a violent tremor at seven P.M. on June 7, 1917. The roof of the house was damaged, and a torrential rain completed the tragedy. The entire city of San Salvador lay in ruins. I think that was the strongest and most destructive earthquake that that region has suffered in historical times.

My grandmother Doña Magdalena Etcheverrie de Arthés was the only child of a lady who would have been of the same name, who was Chatelaine of the Castle of Saint Jean de Luz, on the shores of the Gulf of Gascony, Bas-Pyreness, France. The castle served as a resort where members of the French nobility went on their vacations.

According to family tradition, the Chatelaine said that the father of the daughter Doña Magdalena was a duke of the House of Bourbon, who at that time was vacationing in the Castle. I have not been able to remember the name of the duke. But the archives of the Castle must have the name of the lady surnamed Etcheverrie, who was Chatelaine about the middle of the nineteenth century. And there should appear in the civil records the date of the birth of my grandmother Doña Magdalena Etcheverrie. And it is possible that there may have remained in the register of the castle the name of the Duke who came vacationing some nine months previously. I regret having forgotten.

Doña Magdalena Etcheverrie and her mother arrived in Guatemala shortly before another Frenchman arrived there also, Don Guillermo Arthés. There they met and were married. One of her daughters, Doña Amelie Arthés Etcheverrie, married the gentleman Don Jorge Lardé Bourdon in San Salvador, as was above recorded.

The Lardé Arthés Brothers

𝕿he first children that my parents had, as we explained, were Jorge, Coralie, and Luis. Then were born in that order, Alice, Maria, Carlos, Enrique (the author of this work), and Zelie. On the death of our father Don Jorge, our mother Doña Amelie married Don José del Carmen Rivas, and to that wedlock two more children were born, José and Guillermo. A while later, in 1911, our mother died and the ten of us were left orphans, the oldest, Jorge, being twenty, and the youngest four years of age.

Thereafter the ten of us continued to live together, each giving support to the other, until we had seen our way happily clear of difficulties. Our salvation was the example that our parents had set of high moral standards and self-cultivation, and the will to excellence that they knew how to inculcate. May God glorify them. Blessed, blessed be their souls.

My father Don Jorge and my mother Doña Amelie were very loving with all of us. Despite the difficult circumstances they had to overcome, they were a model husband and wife, and father and mother. They raised us with the wisdom of their teachings, and above all by their example. So great was the will to excellence that they bestowed on us, that despite our having been orphaned so young, all of us succeeded in completing a professional career, and in achieving distinction by our contribution to national culture.

My older brother Don Jorge Lardé Arthés achieved exceptional prominence, his tomb having been declared a "National Monument of the Republic of El Salvador" by decree of the Legislative Assembly, dated June 30, 1948. On his tomb was placed a memorial tablet with the words: "The National Assembly of the Republic Consecrates as National Monument of El Salvador the Tomb of the Wise Professor Jorge Lardé 21 IX 1891 - 23 VIII 1928. A tribute from the Fatherland El Salvador, Central America."

When he died, the well known journalist, author, and philosopher Don Alberto Masferrer wrote: "Death has taken this day, in the life of Lardé, a force that will long be irreplaceable. A fervent soul, an inquiring mind, a restless spirit, Lardé fulfilled in every moment of his intelligent life an impassioned drive to investigate truth, to reveal her, and disseminate her." His powerful influence on Salvadoran culture was such that we could fill many a page quoting eulogies of his life-work, written by the most distinguished of the journalists, educators, and educational institutions of El Salvador.

In 1978, by decree of the Legislative Assembly of El Salvador, my sister Doña Alice Lardé de Venturino was elected Representative of Salvadoran Women in the International Women's Year. She has been distinguished by her literary, scientific, and educational work, as may be found in the article, "A Salvadoran Woman of International Prestige," published in the *Diario Latino* (San Salvador, March 4, 1976). In recognition of her intensive cultural work, the United Women of America named her "Woman of the Americas, 1979" in a ceremony in New York, October 27, 1979.

My sister Doña Zelie Lardé Arthés de Salarrué, wife of the great Salvadoran writer Salvador Salazar Arrué, best known under his pseudonym, Salarrué, devoted herself like her husband to literature and art. She has left oil paintings in an ingenuous style, and a large number of dolls in regional style. In an article, "Rosa Blanca Para un Doble Aniversario," published in *La Prensa Gráfica* (San Salvador) on November 27, 1976, one of her daughters, María Teresa, better known as Maya Salarrué, writes of her mother: "The true mother of Salarrué, the man of letters, the poet, was his virtuous wife, as he acknowledged on a day full of sweetness of emotion. The saying that behind every great man there is always a great woman found here its more perfect illustration."

My brother Doctor Luis Lardé Arthés studied industrial engineering in the Ecole d'Arts et Métiers in Angers, France, but did not complete his studies because the school was temporarily closed by the First World War. Returning to El Salvador, he studied and obtained his doctorate in the School of Dentistry. Aside from becoming eminent within his profession, he devoted some of his time to the teaching of mathematics.

My brother Dr. Carlos Lardé Arthés, a surgeon at the School of Medicine of the University of El Salvador, did post-graduate studies at John Hopkins University in Baltimore as Fellow of the Rockefeller Foundation, and in the Sorbonne at Paris. He was a Medical Doctor and a Doctor of Public Health. Besides having worked since his youth in my country's teaching faculty, he pursued his medical career and became General Director of Public Health. His son, Don Carlos Lardé B., who is also quite well educated, has devoted himself to commerce.

My brothers Doctor José Rivas Arthés, dental surgeon, and Don Guillermo Rivas Arthés, public accountant (besides their respective professions), likewise distinguished themselves in our teaching faculty. Finally, my sisters Coralie and María died too early to have had the time to finish their education.

A Family of Teachers, Artists, and Researchers

𝕴n his book *Escuelas y Maestros de El Salvador* (San Salvador, Editorial Ahora, 1963), my former professor, Don Saúl Flores, wrote in the article entitled "Professor Enrique Lardé,"

The Lardé family is one of teachers, artists, and researchers.

Jorge, the eldest, was a great professor and an excellent researcher. Archeology, seismology, and history were fecund fields to his inquiries; and his premature death cut progress short in many of these disciplines in our country. As a professor he is remembered with fondness by all of his former students.

His wife Doña Benigna, is a magnificent teacher, self-denying and perseverant.

Luis was professor of mathematics in the National Institute and in many private schools for many years.

Zelie, the wife of Salarrué, is an exquisite artist; she performs on the cittern, writes verses, composes music, and has very deft fingers in producing her well-known native dolls.

Alice is an inspired poetess, a great researcher and a teacher of great merit. She has been applauded by eminent poets, writers, and men of science as a truly exceptional woman.

Carlos and Enrique, our former students, were likewise professors; Enrique more truly so than Carlos, once the latter took up his professional medical duties in earnest.

Enrique was mathematics professor in the Instituto Nacional, mathematics professor in the Liceo Moderno and the Colegio García Flamenco, and director of the Instituto de Secundaria de Oriente. He had a strong vocation as a teacher; he loved to put together, working with his students, the aids and equipment needed for practice and experimentation in his classes.

Later he came to devote himself to philosophical studies. He now lives in the United States, with little opportunity, unfortunately, to teach.

A while back the newspapers in the Capital (San Salvador) reviewed his book *La Cábala de los Atlantes*.

His former students and fellow workers at the Colegio García Flamenco remember him with affection. (p. 398).

ESPIRAL - A Magazine

We quote the following from an article called "Amigos en el Tiempo," written by Professor Don Salvador Cañas, which appeared in *La Prensa Gráfica* (San Salvador, Dec. 18, 1956):

Seeing him brought to mind the moments of reverie, contending for ideals, that at that time we viewed as unattainable. Ardent with lyric emotion, Enrique Lardé founded, together with Miguel Angel Chacón, the literary magazine *Espiral*.

Intellectuals of worth collaborated in its publication. They were demanding, perhaps too demanding; they published nothing, whether prose or verse, mediocre. To accept and to publish was to honor. It was in *Espiral* that Salarrué began his stupendous artistic career. Others, like Julia and Tula Van Severen, Miguel Angel and Alfredo Espino, Julio Enrique Avila, Carlos Bustamante, added luster to its pages; Juan Ramón Uriarte, an iconoclast artist for novelty in poetry and literature, acclaimed each issue of the journal with the fiery gusto of a critic and aesthete. *Espiral* revealed an excitement, thoughtfulness, and aspiration in the landscape of Salvadoran letters.

But the area where the personality of Enrique Lardé would make its most esteemed and extensive conquests was the domain of education. As professor of mathematics and physics he served in many education centers, both public and private. We were closely associated with him as such in the Colegio García Flamenco. This school, very dear to our heart, owes him a debt for his presence as teacher and as friend. In its triumphs, but even more in its moments of sorrow and doubt, such as all new endeavors must suffer, he remained firm and ingenuous. He consecrated a portion of his highly productive life to García Flamenco. With his exemplary virtue - and why not say so? - he fulfilled the obligation of a faculty member scrupulously without a pennyworth of remuneration, for the College lacked the funds to meet its own needs. In the annals of the faculty's history at García Flamenco, Enrique Lardé, like Don Bernardino Villamariona, is a figure worthy of respect and deeply moving memories.

The writer and deep thinker Don Juan Ulloa in the article, "Maestro y Filósofo Doctor Enrique Lardé," *Diario Latino* (San Salvador, September 28, 1966), says among other things:

And now we would like to bring up another value in Salvadoran culture: Enrique Lardé. Since we were quite young we knew him as a teacher. He taught courses in public and private colleges. In those days we saw him as a young instructor selling his promissory notes payable by the national treasury, at half their face value, for that was in the time of Presidents Meléndez and Quiñonez, when no civil servant was paid directly and, of course, under pressure of hunger one had to sacrifice one's salary and accept fifty for a hundred. And with so small an income Enrique Lardé helped out his family and paid by fits and starts for his own professional training.

With Miguel Angel Chacón he edited a literary magazine that they called *Espiral*. This publication enjoyed a high prestige around 1924-25. It was that magazine that first published Ramón de Nufio, Arturo R. Castro,

Francisco Miranda Ruano, the Espino brothers (Alfredo
y Miguel Angel), Claudia Lars and a number of other
writers and poets.

The sale of promissory notes, to which Don Juan Ulloa refers,
was a private business run by certain presidents of the country. It
consisted in not paying those on the public payroll directly, especially
not the teachers, in order that they might be forced to sell the
promissory notes at a sharp discount, to designated agents. These
agents in turn were immediately reimbursed the full value by the
treasury, so that they made a hundred percent profit on the deal. The
greater part of this profit was kicked back to the President of the
Republic, and a small percent was kept by the agents. This private
business reached inhuman proportions under President Alfonso
Quiñonez Molina, when civil servants lived on half-pay. The
Meritorious President General Maximiliano Hernández Martínez
put an end to this practice once and for all on the day he took office.

The remark that "With so small an income Enrique Lardé
helped out his family" refers to my having to support, back in those
days, my two sisters Alice and Zelie, who were unmarried, and my
younger brothers José and Guillermo, who were still in school.

The Hacienda Asino

My parents, Don Jorge y Doña Amelie, owned an hacienda
by the shores of Lake Ilopango where they took up
farming, ranching, cheese-making, and lime-quarrying.
My family was staying at the hacienda when I was born prematurely,
in the seventh month. I was born very small, but managed to live
and grow.

They say that as soon as I was a toddler I would always head for
the shore of the lake to catch up and eat *chimbolos*, a kind of tiny native
fish, or else to the bull's corral. I used to catch up by hand and deftly
swallow the chimbolo, which is very small and swims in shallows
near the water's edge. Then I would catch another, and although I
was told that that was naughty, I always would head back to catch
and eat live chimbolos. I probably sensed that my diet lacked
sufficient proteins, and above all those vitamins and minerals that
the live chimbolos could supply me with. What is certain is that I

managed to survive, despite the deficiencies of my puny body.

All this was in El Salvador in the first year of this century, when the instincts of a child of a few months knew more about the nutritional value of vitamins than did all living medical authorities on earth. When I did not need some raw chimbolos, I would go to the bull's corral. It was a beast much feared by the stockmen, because it immediately charged with fury at anything that dared intrude into its corral. But I dared to go in, stooping under the railings, and go up to the bull, and play under its legs. The ferocious bull and I played together. We became pals.

These anecdotes serve as prologue to the article that follows — "Enrique Lardé" by Don Saúl Flores, which appeared in the *Diario Latino* (San Salvador, December 29, 1956):

> Enrique Lardé is back amongst us; he returns to the homeland after many years away; his return brings us much happiness. He was our student in the Instituto Nacional General Francisco Menéndez.
>
> He is the youngest brother of the Lardé family: Jorge, Carlos, Luis, Alice, Zelie, and Enrique.
>
> Alice has skillfully drawn for us, in a lovely lyric, the life of the Lardé family in Asino; one of her loveliest recollections is about Enrique the youngest brother:

> And then old Mayflower, the bull
> Who made us shiver with fear
> While bellowing, whom nobody,
> But nobody came near!
>
> A right uncouth, fierce, surly bull
> Who learned the social graces
> Only the day my youngest brother
> Was playing at his feet.
>
> How humble those devouring eyes,
> How kindly then his bearing;
> It seemed a churlish animal
> Shared goodness like a man's.
>
> Beloved Asino, my Asino!
> Memories crowd on me
> The more tumultuously today,

In that I may never return.

Enrique grew, obtained his baccalaureate, but a family vocation led him into the teaching profession. He was a teacher and one hundred per cent a teacher. We always remember his generous endeavors to illustrate his physics lectures with apparatuses that he improvised. He is moreover the author of a standard history of Central America and of a syllabus for a course of logic.

After many years of endeavor, he left the homeland in search of a situation better suited to develop his personality.

He has lived many years in New York.

Now his thought has matured and now he offers us as the fruit of his reading and deep meditations a philosophical doctrine that he deems highly necessary for our youth.

Let all warmly hail the Salvadoran Professor and wish him a pleasant stay on his native land.

Enrique Rafael or Juan Bautista

When I was born, the young lieutenant Henri Honoré Giraud asked if he might be my godfather, and suggested that I be called Enrique Rafael — Enrique in his own honor, and Rafael in honor of the great painter Raphael Sanzio, of whom my godfather was a great admirer. Our father Don Jorge Lardé Bourdon had proposed calling me Juan Bautista, but finally he accepted the name that my godfather proposed.

That explains why my godfather Henri Honoré Giraud proposed that they call me Enrique Rafael, but not why my adoptive father Don Jorge Lardé Bourdon suggested the name Juan Bautista. It was because he was a great admirer of Jean-Baptiste de Monet, Chevalier de Lamarck, the author of the original theory of the evolution of the species.

I have said that his library, which we inherited, was excellent. It included books of physics, astronomy, and philosophy, but what prevailed there were books on natural history. Among these, a number of beautifully illustrated books stood out, dealing with two theories of evolution, the theory as it stood after Darwin mutilated it, and the original theory as it was expounded by Jean-Baptiste de Monet, Chevalier de Lamarck.

If the most outstanding portion of the whole library, whether for abundance or for the quality of the works, was what dealt with the theory of evolution, then clearly our father was very interested in those theories. And I suspect that the theory of Lamarck fascinated him above all because it was at once scientific and philosophical, and because it was grounded alike in physical and objective facts, and in those mental and subjective facts that are, in reality, the causes of evolution. It seems clear that Darwin was not able to observe the mental facts and the decisive influence that mental forces have on the transformation of the species. This is why Darwin mutilated Lamarck's theory of evolution, eliminating what he failed to understand, and retaining only the materialist element in Lamarck. This mutilated and false theory of evolution is the Darwinism generally accepted by contemporary materialism.

Moreover, the theory of Lamarck is in complete accord with the teaching in the Bible, and that answered well to the temperament and views of our father, who probably was a monastic librarian in various of his previous incarnations. This explains his desire that I might be called Juan Bautista. It may well have also been a factor that his maternal grandfather was called Juan Bautista Bourdon. But my godfather's wish prevailed, and that is how I was registered in the municipal archives under the name of Enrique Rafael.

President Manuel Enrique Araujo

A good friend of the Lardé Arthés family and therefore of Don Justo Armas, was Dr. Manuel Enrique Araujo, who was President of El Salvador from March 1, 1911 to February 9, 1913. Toward the end of 1911, when I was twelve years old, I was crossing the "Finca Modelo" or "Model Farm," when the presidential coach came towards me. It stopped for a moment and the President turned towards me and said, "Little Lardé!" He reached out his hand to help me onto the coach, and gave me a ride around the farm. He asked me about each of my brothers. Then he spoke to me about my parents, Don Jorge Lardé and Doña Amelie Arthés de Lardé, and about several friends of the family. Finally he left me at the same spot where he had invited me to share a ride with him, and went on his way.

This clearly would not have happened had the President not been a close friend of my parents, as he was of my godfather, of Don Anselmo Bellegarrigue Bailly, of Colonel Julio Bias, and of Don Justo Armas, whom he had known since he arrived in El Salvador a dozen years earlier.

Don Anselmo Bellegarrigue Bailly
(October 16, 1861 - May or March 30, 1924 or 1925)

*A*s for my father-in-law Don Anselmo Bellegarrigue Bailly, a good friend of Don Justo Armas, I remember a curious anecdote that illustrates the ability to see things with senses other than the bodily ones. It is the more interesting because there is scarcely anyone who cannot remember an incident in his own life, which, if properly analyzed, reveals this strange ability to see or sense the presence of things that are not immediately before one's eyes.

Don Anselmo would have been about twenty, his studies in Paris over and back in El Salvador, when his mother Doña Catherine Bailly de Bellegarrigue told him that he would now have to find himself a means of earning a living.

Being somewhat at a loss, and without the foggiest idea of what sort of work he could do, he left the house and set out towards the town's center. Soon after he set out he saw a scrap of newspaper windblown along the road and he bent down and picked it up without thinking. He could make out under the mud stains that "the price of caoutchouc has soared to record levels in the international markets."

This newspaper report meant less than nothing to him because in those days, India-rubber or caoutchouc was a product no one had heard of, but the sentence kept spinning in front of his eyes, even as he kept walking. At length he found himself in front of the shop of his friend, Don Juan Balette, and asked him about it. What is caoutchouc? What's it good for? From what is it made or extracted?

Is there any in El Salvador? How does one go about selling it? A few weeks later he had set up a concern for exploiting the caoutchouc in the trees of the virgin forests in the La Paz Department, and so was on his way to his first fortune.

The strange occurrence long intrigued him. Why did he bend down to pick up precisely that scrap of dirty paper windblown along the gutter, an act entirely unbecoming to his upbringing? Why did that sentence about caoutchouc, a product he had never heard of, keep dancing before his eyes? What led him, who had not where, to walk directly to his friend Balette's place, perhaps the only person in San Salvador in those days who chanced to know all relevant data? Doubtless some other "I," his subconscious double, which could use the subtlest powers of the organs of vision, saw the problem as a whole and in detail. And, to communicate the vision with his waking consciousness, he was compelled to stoop to pick that scrap of paper out of the gutter.

My father-in-law was the son of Dr. Jacques Marie Anselme Bellegarrigue, a law professor at the Sorbonne, and Doña Catherine Bailly de Bellegarrigue.

Doctor Jacques Marie Anselme Bellegarrigue
(March 26, 1813 - ?)

WIhen he was a student, Dr. Anselme Bellegarrigue had difficulty understanding advanced mathematics, and could not solve the problems his professor assigned him. But it would happen that after some time he would find on his table, in his handwriting, papers with the solutions to even the most complex problems. He could not at all recall having worked during the night, nor having gotten up, nor having even dreamed that he was working. Nevertheless, the papers were there all written out, proof that at night, with a consciousness other than waking consciousness, he had solved those problems. His bachelor degree from the Academie de Toulous is dated November 7, 1834. There was no doubt about his ability to pursue his studies in mathematics, but he was missing something which prevented the ability to join his talents with his everyday consciousness and he found that something only gradually by thinking over such strange phenomena.

The story is not unfamiliar. The great Paganini had a similar experience, that of waking one morning to find at the head-board of his bed a sonata that he had written asleep, which he therefore called "The Devil's Sonata." Such finding of solutions unawares, which is not uncommon among highly-evolved persons, discloses the great treasures that they carry in their subconscious, treasures that allow them to triumph in the most difficult circumstances, such as those which Archduke Rudolf had to face at Mayerling or in the Straits of Magellan.

While he was a law professor in the Sorbonne, Dr. Anselme Bellegarrigue fell in love with one of his students, Mlle. Catherine Bailly, and married her. A little later they and their son Anselmo went to live in El Salvador. There Dr. Bellegarrigue founded the Faculty of Law and Social Sciences of the University of El Salvador, of which he was the first Dean.

The Astronomer Jean Sylvain Bailly

Mlle. Catherine Bailly was the daughter of Dr. George Bailly, lawyer, who was in turn son of Alexandre Bailly, a mechanical engineer. Alexandre was the brother of Jacques Bailly, painter and writer, and of the astronomer Jean Sylvain Bailly (1736-1793). When Jean Bailly was guillotined, Alexandre left Paris for Dijon, and there established his household.

Jean Sylvain Bailly, uncle of Mlle. Catherine Bailly's father, was an astronomer and politician. He computed the orbit of Halley's comet, was President of the Constitutional Assembly, and afterwards was Mayor of Paris. That was during the French Revolution, when the emotions of the mob prevailed, and the guillotine was much in the order of the day. The great astronomer and politician was guillotined in 1793. Had he been forewarned, he would have been able to escape in disguise, or perhaps in a wine tun, like Don Elois Martín Lardé.

The Quintanilla Family

My wife, Doña Marina Bellegarrigue de Quintanilla, is the daughter of Don Anselmo Bellegarrigue Bailly and of Doña Ercilia de Quintanilla y Abarca. Doña Ercilia was the daughter of Don Ercilio de Quintanilla and Doña Antonia Abarca Rodríguez. Don Ercilio de Quintanilla was a descendant of Don Bartolomé de Quintanilla, a member of one of the fifty families that founded the Noble City of San Vicente de Austria, El Salvador, on December 26, 1635.

Don Juan de Quintanilla and Don Antonio de Quintanilla, who arrived in El Salvador in the age of the conquistadores, were of the Spanish nobility. Don Antonio de Quintanilla was the uncle of Don Bartolomé.

Doña Antonia Abarca Rodríguez was the daughter of Don Juan Abarca and of Doña Dolores Rodríguez, who were both descendants of the fifty founding families of San Vicente. The Abarcas of El Salvador were descended from an illustrious Aragonese family that included men of letters, clergymen, politicians, and so forth.

Doña Dolores Rodríguez was of the family of the priests, the Rodríguez fathers, who number among the fathers of the independence of Central America.

One member of the distinguished de Quintanilla family was Don Francisco de Quintanilla (1699-1769), who was not only *Alcalde Mayor* of the tribunal of the Holy Office, but also *Alcalde Provincial y Regidor* (a provincial governor appointed by the Crown) of the Noble District Council of the Villa (now City) of San Vicente. It was with his strong financial backing that construction was begun of the Church of the Virgin of the Pillar, in San Vicente, in 1762. After his death, his three daughters covered the expenses necessary for completing the construction of that church, whose first chaplain was Father Felix de Quintanilla, of the same family.

Many living descendants of the Bellegarrigue, Bailly, Quintanilla, and Abarca families have attained prominence by their professional, cultural, or business activities. Of these I will name only one more, Monsignor Pedro Arnoldo Aparicio de Quintanilla, presently Bishop of the City of San Vicente de Austria y Lorenzana.

The Psychological Heritage

n this age of materialism, science tries to explain all spiritual phenomena, whether normal or otherwise, as resulting from the anatomical constitution of the body, as in health or illness. The human body does, of course, obey the same biological laws as do all other organisms, including the genetic ones. But when one knows from personal experience that the bodies of men are the instruments of the spirit, one understands that the more advanced spirits tend to incarnate into appropriate bodies; and one likewise understands the force of attraction that those bodies exercise upon the spirits that can best make use of them.

It is like the mutual attraction between Stradivarius violins and virtuoso violinists. And for this reason it has been said that parents, when they engender bodies that are of greater or lesser gifts, are choosing their offspring — that is to say, the character of those spirits that are to incarnate those bodies. And that children, by the way in which they conducted themselves, whether well or ill, in their previous lives, select their parents. There is a parallel evolution of bodies and souls, and a mutual attraction between bodies and those spirits that can make use of them, whether as instruments through which to display great qualities of high vocations, or as bodies fit to revel in the basest passions when given free rein.

In the family of Johann Sebastian Bach there were more than thirteen musicians in five generations. In three generations of the Swiss family Bernouilli there were at least eight renowned mathematicians. Lenz made a study which is still quoted. He found that the incidence of exceptional gifts and talents in well-known exceptional families is about twelve hundred times greater than average. The same proportion has been found in the inheritance of marked moral defect. A high proportion of the descendants of these moral delinquents show the same traits as do their ancestors.

So we can say that although the merits of a person generally depend on his presence, morality, intelligence, plans, and will-power, it also depends, to an even greater degree, on his heredity. In other words, personal merit is enhanced or weakened proportionally to the support that it receives from the inclinations, culture, and activities of one's ancestors. These mysterious forces exist even if we know nothing about their existence and even if we cannot understand them in logical form.

That is why every society inevitably tends to develop a more or less well-defined class structure. This division into classes, with its implied hereditary advantages, cannot but be beneficial to society as a whole.

Not All Men Are Born Equal

𝕿he belief, then, that all men are equal and that therefore all have the same rights, is entirely absurd. Rights are not innate. They are not presents. They are the result of correct observance of duty. Duty comes first. Rights can be lost. There are great differences, profound differences among men at the moment of birth. Some are born intelligent, even geniuses, and others are born stupid as can be. Some are born to lead and others to obey.

For centuries, since they first built upon a craggy height, in the mid tenth century, the famous Falcon Castle, or Habsburg (its original name was Habichtsburg), near where the Aar debouched into the Rhine, the Habsburgs came into the world with high leadership abilities, so much so as to have become the most distinguished among all the reigning families of Europe.

It was this extraordinary and inexplicable spiritual force of the Habsburgs that held together under central rule, and for centuries, an empire compounded of the most varied ethnic elements. And it was the Habsburg Empire, located at the heart of the continent, that saved European civilization from the constant threat posed by the fanaticism, backed by brute force, of the Russians and Turks such as they then were. And that spiritual force of the Habsburgs was the reason why Vienna became one of the most important of world cultural centers.

The craggy height on which the Falcon Castle or Habsburg was built, and its name, stand as a symbol of the Habsburgs themselves who always maintained themselves in the loftiest heights of European society. And they maintained their falcon spirit even in those times when they had to lead a solitary life. Spiritual falcons are born to fly and see from the heights all that takes place on the level plains of human societies, and so earn the skill to guide them, whether in their present or in some future incarnation. But whoever is born in an honorable family, should make his conduct accord with the highest to conserve the noble traditions of the family, and to transmit them to his heirs.

When Erasmus of Rotterdam was appointed tutor of the young prince, who later became the Great Charles V of the Holy Roman Empire and I of Spain, he wrote the book *The Education of a Christian Prince.* Thereafter all the Habsburgs were educated in the spirit of Erasmus' teachings, which sought to inculcate a Christian humanism free of all polemical theology. The spirit of Erasmus, intensely Christian but always independent of clerical dogmatism, has a continuing influence upon all the Habsburgs, including the Archduke Rudolf, and upon his son, the author of this memoir.

The Statistics Of Reincarnation

𝕿here is an apparent contradiction between our not having been born equal and the view that we all are equal because we all are the sons of God. But there is not a real contradiction if we accept the doctrine of reincarnation. In this analysis we must consider both the age in years and the age in reincarnations.

According to the number of incarnations, and regardless of their present age in years, there are old people, young people, and children.

All men were created equal in Paradise, as spiritual beings, but not all at the same time. Some were created in remote times, and have already incarnated repeatedly. Others have been created only recently, and they are incarnating for the first, second, or third time. These differences in number of incarnations are reflected in the greater or lesser degree of spiritual maturity. All distinguished persons, of advanced spiritual maturity, regardless of their age in years, are "the elders," because they have incarnated a great number of times.

The bulk of the population, the masses, are in a primitive state. They have the innocence and ignorance proper to Paradise. They have strong propensities to succumb to all kinds of temptations. They easily let themselves be dragged along by the demagogues who know how to awaken their baser appetites. Regardless of their age in years, these ignorant and innocent people are "the children," because they have incarnated only a few times.

Spiritual beings created in Paradise cannot incarnate unless there are bodies available to receive them. The fact that the world population has doubled during the last one hundred years proves that one half of such population is incarnating for the first time, because never before were there enough bodies for all who are now living. They are "the newly born" among the people of a country.

To repeat, according to statistics, one-half of the world population, and roughly one-half of the population of each country, is incarnating for the first time. Another fourth is reincarnating for the second, third, or fourth time. These three-fourths of the population are "the children," and as children, for their own benefit and for the benefit of the whole country, are expected to obey even if as yet they do not understand.

Only a small number of the remaining fourth are spiritually mature. These constitute the upper social classes, the rulers of the country, the professionals, the managers of important private enterprises, the great artists, the great scientists, the officers of the army, the priests, and other distinguished persons. We can understand the great wisdom and great justice of God if we acknowledge that the inequalities are based not only on age in years, but also on acquired understanding and on age in reincarnations, or age in centuries.

The inequalities based on biological maturity distinguish among babies, children, adolescents, adults, and old people. So do inequalities in the different grades at school, from kindergarten to doctoral studies. These differences reflect themselves in social levels, related to maturity of understanding.

Inequalities due to reincarnations are reflected in the differences between high society and the masses, between families of geniuses and those of ordinary people. Social classes have a tendency to perpetuate themselves because the spiritually mature most often are born in distinguished families, and ordinary people in plebeian families. And the stability of the families perpetuate the classes. That explains the great spiritual qualities and high social status characteristic of the members of the Habsburg family, and other noble families.

Don Julio Bias

owards the end of 1910 I completed my studies in primary school and passed my entrance examination for the National Institute. Two or three months later, on her deathbed, my mother told me among other things that she died contented that I was on the way towards obtaining my baccalaureate. She added: "When you cannot help it, then study by day and work nights, or study at night and work days, but never interrupt your studies so long as you live." I am pleased that I have fulfilled entirely the sum of her recommendations.

Soon afterwards the classes for the new year began at the National Institute. I found myself in very strange surroundings. The professors were for the most part incompetent, and the students informal, undisciplined, uncouth, and vicious. Many of them took to smoking even in the classrooms, and even came with hip flasks to get themselves drunk. Some even came with guns in their holsters. The guards pretended that they did not notice. And it was difficult to understand the baseborn language that they slanged each other in.

Fortunately, not two months had passed in the academic year when on March 1, 1911, Dr. Manuel Enrique Araujo took over as President of the Republic, and among the first things he did was to appoint Colonel Julio Bias as Director of the National Institute. Don Julio Bias, a man of wide culture and a graduate of the Military Academy of Saint Cyr, was in rather serious economic straits. He was earning his living as the foreman of a gang of farm workers, extracting caoutchouc in the forests of the Department of La Paz. He went dressed in cotton breeches and blouse, just like the farm-hands.

When the President called him, urgently, to his duties, he had no other clothing with which to go to the Presidential Mansion than his cotton breeches and coarse cotton blouse. President Araujo ordered him to the Institute immediately. He went to familiarize himself with the situation and make his preliminary decisions. He stayed a few hours only, then left. A week later he returned neatly attired with a new cashmere suit. The entire Institute felt that we now finally had a real Director: Iron discipline; No more smokes, no more boose, no more guns; No more fights and rumbles; No more lapses in respect for the professors and the guards.

And the professors... well, then! Since there were none to be found in the country that met his standards and could raise the level of the curriculum, he appointed young persons, intelligent, determined to continue their own studies side by side with their students, until they became full-fledged faculty members. One of them was my older brother Don Jorge Lardé Arthés, who took charge of the classes in philosophy and natural history.

We have said that Don Julio Bias was a member of my parent's family of friends as were my godfather lieutenant Henri Honoré Giraud, Don Anselmo Bellegarrigue Bailly, the future President Araujo, the future Archbishop Belloso y Sánchez, Don Justo Armas, and other distinguished persons. Don Julio, therefore, knew that my father had an excellent library whose core was works on philosophy and above all natural history. He knew that the Lardé Arthés brothers, who remained as orphans, had inherited that library. And he knew that my brother Don Jorge had his baccalaureate. So it was natural to name him professor of philosophy and natural history, and so my brother found his opportunity to launch his brilliant career. That was how my brother, Don Jorge, helped see us all through our difficulties. It may be mentioned that Don Jorge was a friend of Don Justo Armas since he was a child, and that he kept his friendship while he lived.

It was also on Don Julio Bias' recommendation that Don Luis Lardé was granted a scholarship to study engineering in the *Ecole D'Arts et Métiers* at Angers, France. He treated me also with particular deference in guiding my studies. The stimulus that Don Julio Bias imparted to education was extraordinary. Thanks to him the intellectual level of El Salvador was raised considerably. But the improvement on education was too abrupt, and provoked adverse reaction, especially among the families of those students who found themselves unable to graduate with the baccalaureate without dedicating themselves to their studies. Finally, under the new President of the Republic, Don Carlos Meléndez, the Director of the Institute was replaced.

Of the six hundred of us who were first year students in 1911, only four made it to the seventh, or senior year of studies. The four of us who made it, Luis Araujo, Tomás Mena, Luis Edmundo Vásquez, and I, graduated "summa cum laude." Because these four were too small an entering class for the coming academic year at the University, it was decided to also graduate with a baccalaureate those who made it through their sixth and fifth years. Those who made it through the sixth year were graduated with the qualification of "outstanding," and those of the fifth year as "very good." Thereafter the new curriculum was of five years only, as it had been before the times of Don Julio Bias.

The Beginning Of Communism

𝕬 t a very early age, and before World War One broke out, I became acquainted with the doctrines of nineteenth century radicalism, and with the criticisms usually directed against them, by reading books from the private library of my brother Don Jorge. These included some Marx, the anarchist Kropotkin's *The Conquest of Bread,* and other books of the sort. I used to discuss the theories presented by these idealists of communism with Don Jorge. But it is one thing to chat serenely in one's parlor about communism, and quite another to hear a hotheaded communist fighting for his convictions. Some years later, as the war was coming to an end, Farabundo Martí tried to convince me that I should join the ranks of his party. He was unsuccessful. I already knew what sort of thing was up.

After the revolution of October 1917, which Lenin directed against the government that had overthrown Czar Nicolas II, the Salvadoran public began to interest itself in social issues, and especially in political economy. The capitalist and socialist systems were very much talked about. A few intellectuals believed that the world-wide triumph of communism was inevitable. They found proof positive in astute expositions of the dialectic materialism, presented as an irrefutable truth, and in a perfectly logical structure, to trap the unwary. A great many of these youths succumbed to communist propaganda because at that age it is not yet understood that not everything that can be expressed in a logically consistent manner is therefore true.

Don Anselmo Bellegarrigue Bailly was always interested in contemporary European history. In his conversations with Don Justo Armas he would discuss the latest bulletins on the war, and among them those reporting the dire triumphs of Lenin. Monsignor José Alfonso Belloso y Sánchez, an old friend of Don Justo, joined in with such conversations, and I believe that the experience and knowledge enjoyed by so distinguished a person, one who was so catholic and anticommunist as Don Justo, could not but have benefitted the Monsignor. Let's not forget who Don Justo Armas was before he adopted this pseudonym.

The Worldly Paradise

ven as I am writing these notes, in the middle of 1979, the situation in El Salvador has become extremely sensitive because of the activities of the Marxists. To date the Marxists, over the last three years, have been guilty of a number of kidnappings, assassinations, arson, looting, and so forth, to impose by terror the scientific socialist system of Karl Marx. Among those whom they have so far murdered are a distinguished member of the honorable Regalado family, the Minister of Education, Dr. Carlos Antonio Herrera Rebollo, the Minister of Foreign Affairs, Don Mauricio Borgonovo, the Swiss Chargé d'Affairs, Don Hugo Wey, and many more.

Since the days of Farabundo Martí, the communist leaders in El Salvador have told me that the best way to compromise the government and create conditions favorable to the triumph of communism is to provoke incidents in which innocent blood is shed. For that purpose they organize peaceful demonstrations of innocent persons and then two or three comrades start firing shots at whoever represents the public order, and slip away rapidly in the crowd of demonstrators. The object is to have innocent people fall beneath any bullets that officers might fire back in self-defense. Once blood is spilled, indignation becomes inflamed. The communists achieve their objectives. The communists are the guilty ones if innocent blood has been spilled, but their propaganda converts the police and those responsible for public order into villains.

The nucleus of the communist party consists of a small number of criminals who seek to impose their system by terror, murdering anyone who stands out for his general culture, his administrative capacities, or his scientific, artistic, or religious stature, and so forth. They always talk of establishing a worldly paradise, the reign of God on Earth. But when they triumph, that paradise is the reign of terror, oppression, and despair for those who were imprudent yet still alive. Those of the educated who do not flee in time, disappear when the Marxists have triumphed.

Farabundo Martí

I have always suffered vicariously the griefs of others. The relatives of Farabundo Martí, Luna, and Zapata suffered much when, in 1932, the firing-squad shot those three communist leaders. I suffered much because Farabundo was a good friend of mine in spite of our ideologies being diametrically opposed. The fervor with which he wanted to do away with all human suffering always impressed me deeply.

He wanted the zoological community that constitutes mankind to contain only ewes and doves, living in perfect harmony, in brotherhood, everyone loving the others and all helping each other out. To do this, as he said, one must eliminate the tigers, eagles, and jackals that infest our society. In our environment, he would say, these beasts of prey are the rich, the bosses, the professionals, and the priests, and all those higher-ups who take advantage of the innocence of those beneath them.

He thought that they all had to be killed, including everyone related to the predators, so that the urge to exploitation could never arise again — as in Russia they killed not only the Czar but also the entire imperial family. I had suffered much, and imagine Don Justo Armas did too, a few months before that chat with Farabundo, when the Russian communists slew Czar Nicholas II and the entire Romanov family in 1918. The Romanovs, like the other reigning families of Europe, were related to the Habsburgs.

In Russia the communists beheaded, so to speak, everyone whose head stood above the crowd, whether by intellectual attainment or social rank. Their purpose was to level all by cutting heads off. In graphology this communist ideology, which reveals an inferiority complex, can reveal itself, among other ways, in the tendency to write proper names with lower case letters — that is, in the tendency to avoid capitals. I noticed this tendency among the intellectuals who formed the original nucleus of the Salvadoran communists.

Farabundo was a man greatly mistaken who paid with his life for his mistake. He organized the great uprising aimed at levelling Salvadoran society (eliminating capital letters) in order to leave everyone with the same level of culture, the same level of wealth, etc. Fortunately, the communists failed in their purpose thanks to my friend and professor the Meritorious President General Maximiliano Hernández Martínez.

He Denounced Himself

One of Farabundo's closest friends was Dr. José Llerena. Farabundo discussed all his ideals and plans with him, and Dr. Llerena would follow the conversation letting on that he shared in the same ideology and agreed with the plans of Farabundo. Farabundo so confided and trusted in the doctor that on the night of January 21, 1932, he went to the doctor's house and said: "Tonight at midnight, the revolution. We will kill the rich, the professionals, the bosses, the priests, the nuns, all the leaches living off the blood of the proletariate. Stay indoors with your family. Nothing is going to happen to you. I have given explicit orders; no one is to touch you. The rest must die."

And in his enthusiasm he disclosed details about the workers' organizations that would take part in the uprising, as well as which barracks were inclined to join the uprising against the government and support the popular movement once it broke out that night. He insisted that Dr. Llerena stay indoors with his family, then took his leave.

Dr. Llerena found himself that moment facing a case of conscience. He had no choice but to decide between his loyalty to his friend Martí, and his allegiance to his homeland. If he decided for Martí, a multitude of honorable people would die, and among them many of his friends and relatives, and the entire nation would pay the consequences. He made the only right choice.

It was about eight thirty. He left his home and went to report his conversation with Martí to his brother-in-law Dr. Rafael Víctor Castro, who lived a few blocks away. Dr. Castro immediately got into his car, and drove off to repeat everything to his brother, Dr. Manuel Castro Ramírez. Dr. Castro Ramírez immediately drove off in his car for the Presidential Palace, and repeated everything to General Martínez.

General Martínez lost no time in picking up the telephone to speak, one by one, with each of the commanding officers at the army barracks. First he spoke with the commanding officer at the barrack for the artillery, that being the most important army camp, and said: "Colonel, I have spoken with all the other camp commanders at our several barracks. All have given their full support to the government against the revolution organized by Farabundo Martí. You are the only one I still had to phone." It was the same thing, with the same words, with each of the commanding officers at each barracks in the Republic. Of course, he began with those whom Martí had said were compromised in the plot against the government.

Once they knew the plot had been uncovered, the officers who had been compromised panicked, and had some time of it trying to speak naturally as they reaffirmed their loyalty to the President. Someone with the breadth, maturity, and experience of a General Martínez feels at once what the person at the other end of the line feels, however much he might try to hide his feelings. And feelings betray what one is thinking.

General Martínez managed to prevent any uprising by the military, but it was too late to neutralize the farm workers who had already sharpened their machetes. They rushed out like wild beasts to cut heads off, especially in the departments of Ahuachapán and Sonsonate, where the news that the plot had been uncovered arrived too late. The rebellion was stamped out. Many farm workers died.

Back then the government spokesmen said that around one thousand rebels died. The communists, exaggerating the casualties, claimed that three thousand died. In view of all the information that came to my attention in those days, I think most likely that one thousand died, and about two thousand fled and sought safety in Honduras.

A few years later, communist propaganda claimed that nearly ten thousand died. Now, after more than forty years, communist propaganda no longer says that there were three thousand, or ten thousand, but thirty thousand dead. Most likely in another decade they will be talking of three hundred thousand, and later one will hear that on that occasion three million died. But then, some people believe communist propaganda.

The Pastoral Letter Of Monsignor Belloso

During the World War of 1914, we read in the newspapers what was happening in Europe: The communist revolution led by Lenin in 1917; The massacre of the entire Romanov family in 1918, which was followed by the massacre of all outstanding families of Russia that had been unable to escape by flight; The dismemberment of the Habsburg Empire; The dangerous advance of communism worldwide. But in our own homeland, we were eyewitnesses of the intentions of the communists and the methods that they followed to achieve their ends.

Because of Martí, about one thousand farm workers died. But thanks to General Martínez, the professionals, the businessmen, the priests, the nuns, and in general the educated were alive; they would have perished if the mobs that Martí had raised up, had triumphed. Monsignor José Alfonso Belloso y Sánchez took that occasion to publicly praise the actions taken by President Martínez and to condemn the Marxists.

Soon after the uprising, the Monsignor published a pastoral letter to the Salvadoran public. In it, referring to "the recent successes and the excessively inhuman plan of communism," he said: "If one social class agitates against another threatening death and extermination, the right to life and property must be preserved unharmed... REPRESSION IS JUSTIFIED, provided always that it does not exceed necessity, nor go beyond the limits of self-defense."

In the same pastoral letter, referring to Marxism, he said:

In the first place no one has the right to deny to another the enjoyment of worldly goods by unjust means, whether laying hands on weapons and violence, or contriving iniquitous laws, or scheming civil procedures. Class struggle is condemned by the Gospels, by reason, and by the natural sentiment of benevolence that we extend to our neighbors.

The text of the Monsignor Belloso's pastoral letter against Marxism is included in *Mitras Salvadoreñas*, written by my friend Dr. Ramón López Jiménez, and with a prologue by Prof. Jorge Lardé y Larín (San Salvador, Departamento Editorial del Ministerio de Cultura de El Salvador, 1960).

V. The Sacred Psychic Energies

The Magic Hair And The Stooped Back

My brother, Dr. Carlos Lardé Arthés, played with his nephews and other children telling them that everyone has on the crown of his head a magic hair that is connected with the ears. If you pull backwards on that hair, the ears also wag backwards. The children would cry, "Show us!" And my brother would hunt about carefully on his crown, and on finding the magic hair, made his ears wiggle back with each tug on it.

Everyone has that magic hair. The hard part is to find it the first time. So the children would begin to hunt for the magic hair. But soon they would give up before pulling out all the hair on their head. The muscles that move the ears of quadrupeds are atrophied in man. It is no easy task to locate them with the scalpel when practicing dissection in anatomy classes in medical school. But my brother decided to develop them to see if he could succeed in moving his ears. He felt a need to test his will. He succeeded. He persisted with his imagination and his will, putting in the necessary effort day by day. After two or three weeks he felt them beginning to move. He persevered, and succeeded in wagging them magnificently.

From birth, my brother had quite a well-formed body. But I had a tendency to develop an increasingly stooped back, because of the under-development of the chest muscles. My back muscles were so atrophied that however much I might exercise, I could never straighten out the backbone. But at last, after I had reached my sixty seventh year, and was retired, I had leisure to think more about my person. I remembered how my brother developed the all but nonexistent muscle of his ears, and applied the same procedure to my back muscles. I put imagination and will to work and put in the necessary effort. After a few weeks I began to feel the muscles contract. And it did not take long to straighten out a little.

The rest was a matter of time and persistence. There came the moment when the subconscious took over the job without my needing any conscious effort. When I least expected it, the spinal column straightened itself a trifle more, and after a decade, I being seventy-seven, the column was perfectly straight, from atlas to coccyx. This means that the sacrum finally positioned itself so as to follow the same line as the entire backbone.

This process required a considerable change in the form of the vertebrae, to adapt the articular surfaces to the new position. And the development of the thorax further implies the lengthening of the ribs, and the buying of larger size clothing, because shirts and suits no longer will let themselves be buttoned. Let it be clear that I am by no means referring to putting on weight. I speak only of eliminating a spinal curvature and raising a sunken chest, together with an enlargement of the thorax.

I know well that the medical doctors will say this is impossible. After the first forty years of life, they say, the skeleton has reached its maximum development. Thereafter it keeps the same size. Then after sixty it tends to shrink. I am thoroughly aware and I know how that is the general rule. I also studied anatomy, physiology, histology, and other such required courses in the School of Medicine. The shrinking of the skeleton after fifty or sixty is the general rule. But miracles do happen and my body bears witness to this by its considerable and impressive development after sixty-seven, and after I had faced the rigors of life with the shrunken body of a seven-month-premature baby.

This imagination and will, and the feeling of the contraction of the muscles that must be developed, is part of what Lamarck calls the interior sentiment. And this is one of the things that Darwin never was able to understand. When Lamarck points to the role that necessity plays in the evolution of the species, he insists on the supremacy of mind over purely material phenomena. In short, psychological changes conduce organic changes. I have proven as much by the transformation of my own body.

As Lamarck says, the evolution of species is due to the voluntary guidance of the interior sentiment, when faced by a need that must be satisfied. The theory of evolution in Lamarck is theological and not materialist. I will not expand on this since I have dealt with it extensively in *La Cábala de los Atlantes*, published in 1960, and also in the English version which has not yet been published, *Occult Christianity*. Of direct interest are not only the extensive commentaries on Lamarck's theory, but also the elucidation of the views of Descartes with respect to the animal spirit.

He Did Not Rest On His Heels

I remember that Don Justo walked on the front part of the soles of his feet and toes only, the heels always totally raised above ground, and never touching down. Even when he stood without walking, Don Justo remained with his heels totally raised. This was not easy to notice because he wore pants that reached almost to the ground.

When the Archduke was standing, he did not have his legs quite straight, but a trifle bent, so that the knees turned forward and outward. And when walking he progressed with a slight movement of balancing from side to side, and at the same time straight up and down, his head bobbing up and down with each step.

It is the overdevelopment of the balls of the feet, at the base of the big toes that cause the knees to stick out forwards and to the sides, which also causes the lateral swing of the body when walking. The up and down motion of the body is caused by the excessive length of the feet relative to the length of the legs. These organic defects, which were less marked in his father, the Emperor Francis Joseph, are much more exaggerated in his son, the author of this memoir.

The lateral motion is reduced or eliminated by using insoles thicker on the outer side, to compensate for the overdevelopment of the ball on the inner side of the feet. That is, with a special insole, or with special prosthetic shoes. The distal or outer side of the metatarsus should be raised to compensate for the overdeveloped ball. The up and down motion is corrected by increasing the height of the heels.

Many Bourbon Kings of France used rather high heels. They were related to the Habsburgs. And as I said, my mother was the granddaughter of one of the dukes of France. Those kings used rather high heels not out of vanity, as many believe, but to compensate for the above-mentioned defects.

The entire skeleton is interrelated and balanced harmoniously in all its parts and the proper distribution of the weight in the feet is extremely important and affects this harmony. In fact this harmony is affected by the shoes one wears and we all know that there are shoes which feel comfortable and others which wear one out. When the problem is not in the shoe but in the feet themselves, the problem of course is permanent and it manifests itself eventually in the entire skeleton.

When he was still in Austria, Archduke Rudolf suffered on

account of these defects in his feet. That is the length of the feet in proportion to the length of the legs and also the overdevelopment of the balls of the feet. These resulted in a curvature of the spine which was the more pronounced due to the inadequate development of his chest muscles. Specifically, these combined defects exaggerate the curvature of the cervical, dorsal, and lumbar regions, as also the angle of the sacrum and the last lumbar vertebrae.

The Archduke tried to correct his spinal curvature with the weight of a knapsack on his back during his alpine excursions. This knapsack was supported by a harness of straps meant to thrust the shoulders back and the chest forward into the correct posture. If not the knapsack, he carried a hunting rifle on his back also with the straps around each of the shoulders, so as to thrust them back. But this did not work for him, any more than I was helped by a devise of straps especially designed for this purpose.

Moreover, when the Archduke was preoccupied, he would stand gazing into the distance out of the window, with his body leaning a trifle forward, and his hands clasped behind his back. This same instinctive gesture was habitual with His Majesty Francis Joseph, and exaggeratedly-so with me.

I recall that toward the end of 1917, having recently received my baccalaureate, I was named history instructor in the Escuela Normal de Varones (Normal School for Boys), which in those days was in Cojutepeque, because in San Salvador there were not any houses left standing suitable for the school after the earthquake of June 7, 1917.

I was much wrapped up in thought because I had to resolve many rather difficult problems in my new stage of life. I was eighteen, and wanted to study medicine in San Salvador. But I had to earn my living at the same time, and help out my sisters and young brothers. My favorite place to stroll was the Central Park of Cojutepeque. When I strolled pensively through the park, I walked leaning a bit forward, face down, with my hands clasped behind my back.

My girlfriends told me to give up the habit of walking that way, hands clasped behind me, but to do so would have required changing my entire skeletal posture, and I could not yet work on that. I did not yet realize that I had to compensate for the disproportion of my feet by using prosthetic devices in my shoes. There was no time to think of such things. All my thought was on studying and earning a living. And so I often walked pensive, leaning a bit forward, face down, with my hands clasped behind my back. This posture was instinctive in both my father, Archduke Rudolf, and the Emperor Francis Joseph.

The Gigantic Effort

We have said that when the Saint Margaret was shipwrecked in the Straits of Magellan, the Archduke managed to survive by holding onto a plank of the downed ship, and remained afloat on the waters. In his despair Don Justo vowed to the Virgin Mary that, if saved, he would walk barefoot forever after. Of course when he made that pledge he did not think of the great sacrifice that it would involve to walk barefoot for the rest of his life. Had his feet been normal, it would not have been so difficult. But with long feet and short legs, it was a different matter. It was necessary to walk on the front part of the soles of his feet and toes only, with his heels totally raised at their maximum, just as he did often when alone in his apartment, back at the palace in Austria.

Thereafter he would not walk barefoot for a few minutes, but for the duration of his life. That implies an enormous sacrifice, a gigantic effort. Being a man of honor, and moreover a truly pious man, he did not for one minute think of breaking his promise to the Virgin. He was determined as ever to keep his word.

Getting into the habit was slow and painful. To walk constantly in that position, it was necessary to develop his foot and leg muscles. He had to straighten out his spinal column. He had to develop his thorax. He had to build up his negligible back muscles. He had to readjust all the articulations to his new posture.

This readjusting of the intervertebral joints means stretching ligaments, tendons, muscles, blood vessels, and nerves. This process is accompanied by more or less painful inflammations, and complications in calcium metabolism, which result in severe cramps both in the voluntary muscles of the body and the involuntary muscles of the digestive tract. Cramps in the esophagus due to calcium deficiency are especially excruciating.

The most severe reaction occurs when the articulation of the sacrum with the fifth lumbar vertebrae is straightened out. This articulation ceases to be at an angle to the general line of the backbone. The stretching of the associated tissues that results produces an inflammation that may prolong itself up to two years, for the entire pelvis must readjust with the sacrum, and the articulations of pelvis and femurs also must suffer. These three articulations form a triangle enclosing the perineum, which likewise becomes inflamed. All this creates a situation of stress which affects the heart. But the Archduke was set to keep his word at any cost. He was an honorable and pious man. After surviving Mayerling and the Straits, he had faith that he would triumph again. And he persevered until he had adapted to the new situation.

The adaptations that were necessary for him to walk barefoot without walking hunched, and without losing the presence and the dignity of a prince, must have been most beneficial. It must also have been good for him to work in the fields, in remote regions of Argentina. Hereafter Don Justo was a strong man, vigorous and broad-shouldered, and he appeared to be of normal stature because his heels were always totally raised. The posture of his feet was almost not noticeable because his pants, neatly pressed, reached to the ground. Generally, of his feet only his robust and vigorous toes were visible.

He Was Not Timid

Remarkable fortitude and great executive abilities were always characteristics of the members of the House of Austria. To this is due the history of the Habsburgs being not just the history of an imperial family but the history of all Europe. It was the general consensus of Viennese society, prior to the campaign of calumnies begun at Mayerling, that this spiritual heritage of the Habsburgs was strongly marked in Archduke Rudolf. He was regarded as highly-endowed in his culture, intelligence, prudence, noble sentiments, and lofty morals.

But this spiritual heritage was in contrast to his weak constitution, partly inherited from his mother, Empress Elizabeth, and partly due to the consanguinity both of his parents and of his grandparents. This weak constitution is to blame if the prudence of the young Archduke was mistaken for timidity. I repeat, the Archduke was not timid but prudent. Archduke Rudolf forcefully rejected the idea of forcing the abdication of the Emperor in favor of the Crown Prince, which is what the liberal leadership suggested to him prior to the tragedy of Mayerling. If he rejected that idea, it was not out of timidity but because he was a man of honor, respectful of the traditions of the family.

The young Archduke was gallant, but not a seducer of both young ladies and married women, as was alleged during the campaign of calumnies launched against him by the clergy and archconservatives of the Empire during the tragedy of Mayerling. Had he been timid, the Archduke would have ended his life in the jail cell of a monastery, as the clergy among the conspirators had planned. Had he been timid, he would not have decided to begin life anew, in completely different circumstances, in a distant land. Had be been timid, he would not have survived the tormenting tragedy of the Straits. And had he been timid, he would not have completely transformed his body during his life in the Argentina Pampas. All this discloses a spirit basically intrepid, energetic, and persevering.

The Archduke had also, as did almost all the members of his family, a great reserve of sacred psychic energies, of that kind of energy which is found latent at the base of the backbone among persons of advanced moral stature, and which come to fruition at the suitable hour. This bone at the base of the spinal column derives its name "sacrum," which means "sacred," from the fact that in its magnetic field these great reserves of sacred psychic energies are latent. With the awakening of these energies the gaze becomes stronger and more penetrating, and one's words reach further and produce greater effects, whether it be the spoken word or the written word.

Naturally once these energies are actualized, one senses other persons with greater clarity. One senses their intentions, honorable or treacherous. One senses what someone at the other end of the telephone is feeling, and on that basis knows also what he is thinking. Moreover, in some circumstances, one senses even in what surroundings that person is, no matter whether he speaks from another place in the same city, or from some more considerable physical distance.

The Archduke's reserves of sacred psychic energies began to awaken during the tragedy of Mayerling. But they did not achieve full actualization until after he succeeded in wholly straightening his spinal column during his stay in remote regions of Argentina. These energies are known always to rise vertically through the magnetic field of the spinal medulla, from the region of the sacrum through the cerebrum, where, by means of the fontanels, they communicate with the sacred energies in one's surroundings.

At first one feels that they reach the fontanelle between the parietal and occipital bones. As the backbone becomes more straight, there comes the moment when the direction of the course changes suddenly to reach the fontanelle between the frontal and parietal bones. Finally, when the backbone is completely straightened out from atlas to coccyx, one feels the sacred psychic energies reach the juncture of the frontal and ethmoid bones, and their effects upon one's surroundings make themselves felt most, especially by means of one's voice and one's gaze.

When the Archduke came to El Salvador, he was a man of very distinguished presence, of a sweet, strong, penetrating gaze, of a convincing voice, of a constitution strong, vigorous, and impressive.

VI. Only the Memory Remains

They Are Dead Now

Much has changed in El Salvador since the early years of this century. The younger generations are strongly materialistic in outlook. Respect for and fear of religion have vanished. Many elements in the Catholic clergy are becoming Marxist. It seems that now the chief concern of men is not to lead the good life in accord with the loftiest precepts of Christianity. Those days are gone. Now the chief concern is money, and more money, and to give no thought to anything but still more money.

Those who knew Don Justo when they were young or as children towards the beginning of this century are now almost all dead, and the few who remain walk with an uncertain step helping themselves with a cane.

Who was Don Justo? The answer now is almost always indirect. "They said that he was... The story goes, he was...." And at best there follow repetitions of the numerous and fabulous legends that grew up around so mysterious a personality. "They say he was Maximilian, Emperor of Mexico... No, he was not Maximilian, but an illegitimate son of Maximilian... No that is not true. I have heard tell that he was the Archduke Luis Victor." And in this manner opinions multiply. What is worth noting is how the memory of Don Justo is always linked with a member of the House of Austria. He was unquestionably Austrian. He knew Belgian culture in depth and the Belgian milieu. He lived a long time in Argentina. He wore a beard very similar to that of the Emperor Francis Joseph. And at official ceremonies and during receptions in the Presidential Palace at the turn of the century, and for some years after, he wore a military jacket identical to that of His Majesty, the emperor Francis Joseph.

What few still know at first hand is that Don Justo Armas was the very Archduke Rudolf. His physiognomy showed it, as did his presence and culture. He was unquestionably the Crown Prince. No one of his generation still lives. Don Jorge Lardé Bourdon and his wife Doña Amelie Arthés Etcheverrie de Lardé are dead — they who first received him and helped him at the opportune moment, when on arrival in El Salvador he had not the least idea of how to find work and earn a living in our country.

My brother Don Jorge Lardé Arthés is dead, who all his life since childhood was a friend of Don Justo. Successive presidents are dead; General Rafael Antonio Gutiérrez, General Tomás Regalado,

General Fernando Figueroa, Dr. Manuel Enrique Araujo, Dr. Pío Romero Bosque — all of them friends of Don Justo. The Arbizú are dead, as are the Arrieta Rossi, Don Anselmo Bellegarrigue Bailly, General Henri Honoré Giraud, Colonel Julio Bias, Doña Adriana Cabrolier with all her brothers, and many others who were good friends of Don Justo at the turn of the century and into this century. Don Justo Armas died on May 29, 1936. Two years later, August 9, 1938, Monsignor Alfonso Belloso y Sánchez died. And finally, in 1978, Don Juan Ulloa died.

In El Salvador today, Don Justo Armas is only a legendary figure. To me, he is a historical personality of the highest importance. What popular imagination has added to his story is interesting. But what interests me is the factual life of Archduke Rudolf, from his first years in the home of their Majesties the Emperor Francis Joseph and the Empress Elizabeth, to his demise in San Salvador, after he had overcome all of the difficulties of his tempestuous life. Of the news articles that have appeared in the Salvadoran press that deal with this legendary figure, I want to translate and comment on two that are important: an interview with Monsignor José Alfonso Belloso y Sánchez, published in *La Prensa* (San Salvador: May 30, 1936) and an article by Don Juan Ulloa, published in *La Prensa Gráfica* (San Salvador: November 4, 1970).

An Interview With Monsignor Belloso

WAS DON JUSTO ARMAS THE BROTHER OF EMPEROR MAXIMILIAN? Monsignor Belloso y Sánchez, who kept up a close friendship with him thinks he was.

One of our reporters went this morning to visit Monsignor Alfonso Belloso y Sánchez, Archbishop of San Salvador, knowing that the Salvadoran high prelate was an old friend of Don Justo Armas, deceased yesterday in this capital and the object of the most curious legends.

In effect, Monsignor Belloso told our reporter that Don Justo Armas was not South American as had been assumed, nor was that his true name. Monsignor Belloso says that Don Justo died at the age of one hundred and forty, having arrived in El Salvador in 1860.

He was of Austrian origin and had studied in Belgium.

In the conversations that Monsignor had with him, he indicated that he had been captain of the ships that supplied ammunition, victuals, and so forth, to the filibusters active in Nicaragua.

When the revolution that overthrew Maximilian had triumphed, Don Justo was in México, where he placed himself under the protection of a family called *Armas,* to escape from the firing squads of the troops under Juárez.

And for his not wearing shoes, Monsignor Belloso says that when Don Justo was running the Atlantic on the way to Cuba, his boat sank, and under duress he made a vow to the Virgin of Mount Carmel that if she saved him he would never again wear formal suits or shoes. A plank came within the reach of Señor Armas, and bore him up as far as a beach in Florida (U.S.A.).

Monsignor Belloso, despite Señor Armas having always refused to disclose his real identity, believes that he was a younger brother of the Austrian Emperor Maximilian. He says he knows him to have kept a diary of his life, in which he detailed the episodes thereof.

Don Justo Armas was fluent in five or six languages and possessed an extensive cultural background.

Naturally the belief of Monsignor Belloso bears every sign of being authentic fact and who knows whether, now that Señor Armas is dead, who here dedicated himself to the hotel business, we may discover that he was a member of the Austrian nobility.

The diary to which Monsignor Belloso refers would in that case shed some light on the matter.

A Commentary On The Interview

 n analysis of the interview above discloses that the reporter for *La Prensa* did not know how to distinguish between what

Monsignor knew first-hand by conversations with Don Justo, from what he imagined to be the case, and from what he picked up second-hand from rumors.

Monsignor says that he was an Austrian who had studied in Belgium. Don Justo was evidently an Austrian, but he did not study in Belgium. The confusion is due to Don Justo speaking as one who was well-informed about Belgium and the Belgian royal family, which would come naturally to one whose wife was the Princess Stephanie, daughter of the King of Belgium.

The rumors that Monsignor Belloso repeats about Don Justo having been captain of ships bearing ammunitions, victuals, etc. (to the filibusters who were battering the peace of Nicaragua) do not make sense. William Walker and his filibusters fought in Nicaragua in 1856-57, over thirty years before the tragedy of Mayerling, and some ten years before the adventure of Maximilian in México. In 1856, Maximilian was only twenty-four, Louis Victor fourteen, and Rudolf was born two years later. None of them could have taken part in those adventures of William Walker.

None of the other archdukes accompanied Maximilian, so that it is not correct to think, as Monsignor Belloso supposes, that Don Justo Armas was the younger brother of Maximilian (in other words the Archduke Louis Victor), and that when the Emperor was captured in Querétaro the young Archduke took shelter with the Armas family to avoid the firing-squads. All that is absurd. It is pure fantasy and no more. Monsignor also says that Don Justo arrived in El Salvador in 1860. That is not so. He arrived in September 1898.

What Monsignor says about Don Justo dedicating himself to the hotel business is equally false. Never in his life did Don Justo dedicate himself to the hotel business. But with the help of my parents, Don Jorge Lardé and Doña Amelie Arthés de Lardé, who owned the Hotel Europa, Don Justo launched his small business as caterer for parties and banquets.

Monsignor Belloso says that Don Justo died at the age of 140. Probably he meant to say 104, which is the age that Don Justo would have been in 1936, had he been Maximilian. And if he had been Archduke Louis Victor he would have died at the age of ninety-four. But Don Justo was neither Maximilian nor Louis Victor. Maximilian was executed at Querétaro in 1867, and Archduke Louis Victor died in 1919. Monsignor Belloso, then, like all who have published articles in the Salvadoran press about Don Justo, was not well-informed about historical realities and he mixed fact with fiction.

Monsignor Belloso says that when Don Justo was sailing towards Cuba his boat sank, and that Don Justo, clinging to a plank, managed to make it to the Florida coastline of the United States. Monsignor is clearly getting his facts mixed up. The shipwreck occurred in the Straits of Magellan in mid-August 1890. Monsignor also says that Don Justo made a vow to "the Virgin of Mount Carmel" when he was clinging to a plank, on the ocean. Let us clarify that the vow was made "to the Virgin," as we always knew at my home. But later on, when talking to other people, he added "of Mount Carmel" to suggest what happened to his partner in misfortune, Baroness Maria Vetsera, who was imprisoned for the rest of her life in an austere "Carmelite" monastery.

But what Monsignor Belloso (and others who have published articles on the same subject) have to say, does corroborate in general this much: That Don Justo was a member of the House of Austria, an Archduke. That he had an extensive cultural background, and was fluent in five or six languages, as would be natural to a Habsburg. That he knew Belgium well. That he knew well what life was like in Argentina and neighboring countries, so much so that many in El Salvador thought him a South American. (This opinion was quite natural, since he lived many years in Argentina after the shipwreck in the Straits of Magellan.)

Finally, Monsignor merely wanted to hint at the intimate friendship between Don Justo Armas and my mother Doña Amelie Arthés de Lardé, when he said that Don Justo "dedicated himself to the hotel business." So far as I know, Monsignor is the only person to have said that Don Justo was so involved. He said it knowing it to be false, if his words are taken at face value. What he really meant to say is that my natural father was Don Justo Armas and that my mother was Doña Amelie Arthés de Lardé, owner of the only hotel there was in San Salvador in those days. He did not say so openly from discretion, so that La Prensa might be able to publish what everyone knew in secret.

But Monsignor's allusion was clear enough for people to understand what he wanted to set down for the record. It was obvious that I was the son of Don Justo. Corroborative evidence was provided by both my parents, Don Jorge and Doña Amelie, having black hair and eyes. And all my siblings had brunette or dark brown hair, their eyes grayish or black. None had blue eyes. I alone had quite red hair and the eyes entirely blue, with a ruddy complexion, just like Don Justo. These contrasts between the color of my hair and eyes, and my ruddy complexion, and that of the rest of the family, were well known, and corroborate what Monsignor hints at, and what gossip circulated in secret.

Biographical Data On Monsignor Belloso

onsignor José Alfonso Belloso y Sánchez was born in San Salvador, El Salvador, on November 30, 1873. He studied in the Colegio Pio Americano and the Gregorian Institute at Rome, where he obtained his Ph.D. Later he studied in Paris, at the Seminary of Saint Sulpice. In 1897, he was ordained priest in Lateran Cathedral, Rome, and after his ordination he returned to San Salvador just before Don Justo Armas arrived in that city. In late 1905, he was named Director of the Salvadoran Lyceum in San Salvador.

Monsignor Belloso was anointed Bishop on May 30, 1920, and elected Archbishop on December 19, 1927. Two years after the death of Don Justo Armas, Monsignor Belloso died in Santa Barbara, California, on August 9, 1938, at the age of 75. His mortal remains were sepulchred in the Cathedral of San Salvador.

Note: Almost all the biographical data above provided on Monsignor José Alfonso Belloso y Sánchez was drawn from Dr. Ramón López Jiménez, *Mitras Salvadoreñas* (San Salvador: Departamento de Educación del Ministerio de Cultura de la República de El Salvador, C. A., 1960).

The Life of Don Justo Armas, According To Juan Ulloa

n an article entitled *The Enigmatic Life of Don Justo Armas* (La Prensa Gráfica, San Salvador, November 4, 1970), Don Juan Ulloa says the following:

History, which is like the voice of time, coldly relates the events that have happened to peoples and to men. So does it tell us a little of what happened in México in the year 1864, when France intervened to stifle a civil war and imposed a new empire in the Aztec nation, whose scepter it gave to Archduke Ferdinand Joseph Maximilian, who according to that same history was deposed by Benito Juárez and executed in 1867.

Before the execution, Víctor Hugo sent a letter to the Mexican ruler asking for pardon for that fallen monarch who had no hope left of the earth that might merely receive him. But to this is added one important detail. With the passage of years men have said that the officer in charge of the execution of Maximilian took his hand in farewell and was surprised to receive the famous signal used by Masons to identify themselves to their fellows. This officer was also a Mason, as was Benito Juárez, and had to inform the latter that the man they were to execute was a member of the fraternity. So the problem arose and, with many reservations, he was pardoned, but the Mexican public was always made to believe that the firing squad shot him, and all appearances to that effect were kept up.

The same year, perhaps during the very days that these things took place, a distinguished person, slender, fair of complexion, blue-eyed and red headed, bearing a marvelous resemblance to the emperor condemned to death, landed at one of our ports.

That distinguished person was called among us "Justo Armas." We had the opportunity to know him. He came to live, here in San Salvador, at the address No. 36 (now No. 524) of the Second Orient Street.

Don Justo Armas, the mysterious person who chose never to reveal what family he came from, devoted himself since that time in 1867 to catering banquets given by presidents of the Republic, and it is said of those famous banquets that they were never lacking in the most luxurious silver-ware, the loveliest damask curtains, and the chandeliers of the patriarchal style.

Don Justo came to be so popular that not only did major figures in politics and banking resort to him, but also heads of state paid him visits, such a Barrios, Gutiérrez, Regalado, and so forth.

We visited him once when young to meet him personally and ask if it was true that he went barefoot because of a vow that he had made when he was a passenger aboard a ship sinking on the high seas. He answered with the smile of a great lord... He was very reserved.

When he was at the banquets he always presented himself well-attired. His jackets never had the usual lapels. They were like those military jackets that are buttoned up to the neck.

There are two photographs. In one of them the Emperor Maximilian is mounted on a showy charger. In the other is Don Justo Armas. The resemblance of the two persons remains exact after detailed analysis.

He died here in San Salvador May 29, 1936, at the age of one-hundred-and-four. His mortal remains rest in the mausoleum of the honorable Arbizú Bosque family. This family showed him much esteem when living.

In one of the drawers of his desk, which was always kept under key, two flags were found, laid in a cross, that of Austria and that of Mexico.

Commentary On The Preceding Article

𝕿his article, like all others about Don Justo Armas, contains some truth and much fantasy. In the first place, it says that Don Justo was the Emperor Maximilian. We have already said that this is entirely false (*vide supra*, "He was not Maximilian," pg. 5).

He says that the major figures in Salvadoran politics visited him, such as Presidents Barrios, Gutiérrez, Regalado, and so forth. This is true enough except for Captain General Gerardo Barrios, who was shot by the firing squad on August 29, 1865 — that is, two years before Maximilian was executed in Querétaro, and twenty-three before Don Justo Armas arrived in El Salvador. Barrios accordingly could not have been a friend of Don Justo.

When Don Justo Armas arrived in El Salvador, the President was General Rafael Antonio Gutiérrez. Soon after, on November 14, 1898, General Tomás Regalado succeeded him in power. These two presidents, to show him favor, encouraged Don Justo to organize the banquets at the Presidential Palace. My parents Don Jorge Lardé and

Doña Amelie Arthés de Lardé, also in order to befriend Don Justo (who had arrived in El Salvador in an economically embarrassed state), lent him "the most luxurious silverware, the loveliest damask curtains, and the chandeliers of the patriarchal style" which, according to Don Juan Ulloa, were never lacking in the banquets at the Presidential Palace in those days. We have already referred to this matter (*Supra*, "I Was In On The Secret", pg. 6).

The description of Don Justo is correct. Don Juan Ulloa says that Don Justo was a distinguished person, slender, fair of complexion, blue-eyed and redheaded, bearing a marvelous resemblance to the Emperor Maximilian. He says that when Don Justo presented himself at banquets he was always well-attired. His jacket never had the usual lapels. It had a high collar, buttoned up to the throat, like those that military officers use. To judge by his wearing a beard trimmed in the style of his father's, Emperor Francis Joseph, and by the military jacket of which Don Juan Ulloa tells us, Don Justo doubtless wanted to let it out that he was the Archduke Rudolf, but without saying a word. Don Juan Ulloa also mentions in his article some other details already known to us, such as why he always walked barefoot, the sinking of the ship in which he was sailing, and the two flags, one of México and one of Austria, that were found at his death in the drawer of his desk.

Biographical Data On Juan Ulloa

Don Juan Ulloa Cañas, a man of high lineage, of the family of the great José Simeon Cañas, the liberator of the slaves in Central America, was born in San Vicente, El Salvador, on June 24, 1898, and died in San Salvador on March 12, 1979. He held important political posts, such as Private Secretary to President Engineer Arturo Araujo, Cultural Ataché to the Salvadoran Embassies in México and Guatemala, Deputy to the National Legislative Assembly, Director of the *Diario Oficial* (Official Gazette), and Director of the National Library. Ulloa wrote poems, plays, stories, and essays. He published ten or more volumes.

The critics agree that Juan Ulloa certainly did occupy a place entirely his own among the most brilliant Salvadoran writers. His prolific pen disclosed a vast intellectual background, for he wrote on literature and the physical sciences with the same facility as he did on the great questions of metaphysics.

Note: Almost all the biographical data provided above is taken from Juan Ulloa, *Carbones Encendidos* (San Salvador: Departamento Editorial del Ministerio de Educación de la República de El Salvador, 1972).

The Autobiography Of Don Justo Armas

When she mailed me a photograph of Don Justo taken in the last years of his life, Doña Alicia Arbizú Bosque wrote me that Don Justo never spoke the truth when asked about his family or homeland. He answered evasively and changed the topic to prevent any more questions. As for his life after Mayerling, the only thing known for sure is the information that he gave my mother in the strictest confidence when in San Salvador, in order that I might know it when the time came. In her letter Doña Alicia enclosed a copy of the autobiography contained in Don Justo's will. On seeing the photograph and reading that biography, one reflects on the outcome of that great tragedy of Don Justo Armas' entire life.

When he came to San Salvador, Don Justo wore a beard and a military jacket very like those which his father, Emperor Francis Joseph, also wore. He wanted it known that he was the Archduke Rudolf, but without having to say so. But in his last years, when he expected nothing more out of life, he no longer cared whether anyone knew who he was. The tragic death of his mother and the interminable campaign of slanders directed against him in his homeland, Europe, and the rest of the world, wilted away all joy, all illusion, all desire to live on. That is what his photograph shows.

The portrait shows dignity. It shows high-mindedness. It shows the energy of one who could have been a great emperor. But he did not succeed in becoming one in this incarnation. His talk and his bearing left no possible doubt that he was an Austrian, a Habsburg, that he had lived many years in Argentina, and that he knew Belgium thoroughly. But aside from this, almost everything that was said about him was pure guesswork, much of it based on what Don Justo himself had said, to put off the inquisitive.

To add to the confusion, in his will he writes the following autobiography, which seemingly contradicts everything that is known or that is told about Don Justo:

I am 91 years old (this in 1930). I have never known the name of my parents, nor where I was born, but I remember that in infancy or childhood I used to be in San Antonio, Texas, when it belonged to Mexico, under the guardianship of a lady and an Austrian priest, from whose care I was removed by some Indians, and later, still as a minor, I found myself in Tampico, under the guardianship of a landed Spanish family of much wealth, named *de Armas*, a family which looked after me with much love and affection and which gave me the Christian and the family name that I go by. In my youth, I saw myself always provided with the necessary sufficiencies for life, without knowing for certain who it was that provided them, until I was able to meet my need by my own labor. Since 1860, I have been in this Republic, El Salvador. Since then I have resided in this capital.

It is natural for anyone to try not to think of, and even to erase from his memory, all painful recollections. In certain cases, when one's memories are too painful, complete amnesia may result. This autobiography does not disclose a real amnesia, but a pretended one. It is the culmination of the tactics he had adopted to put the inquisitive off the trail. Nevertheless, we find in the autobiography some ideas quite firmly rooted in the subconscious:

a) That in his infancy or childhood he found himself in a country such that that country belonged to him. That is, he found himself in Austria which in those days was a part of his dominions as Crown Prince. One may observe the word-play and hidden meaning in the phrase, "when it belonged to México," for "when it belonged to *me*." (The word-play is as clear in the Spanish.)

b) That during his infancy or childhood he was under the care of a non-Austrian lady (Elizabeth) and an Austrian priest (Francis Joseph), from whose care he was removed by some Indians. These Indians must be the Jesuits and the Ministers Taaffe and Kalnoky.

c) That in his youth he saw himself always provided with the necessary sufficiencies for life, until he was able to meet his needs by his own labor. This would be in El Salvador, as caterer for feasts and banquets.

d) That for a period of his life, still in his minority, he was in the care of a Spanish family, landed and wealthy, which looked after him with much love and affection. This would be in the Pampas, in remote regions of Argentina, after shipwreck in the Straits of Magellan.

e) That his original name was not Justo Armas. He was indeed the Archduke Rudolf.

f) The allusions to México and Tampico, together with the disdain with which he refers to some Indians, reminds us that he always remembered affectionately his uncle, the Emperor Maximilian, who was defeated and shot by the "Indians" of México. He surely remembered always with tenderness his mother the Empress Elizabeth, his father the Emperor Francis Joseph, and his uncle Emperor Maximilian, as is shown by the two flags, one of Austria and one Mexican, that were found in his desk drawer.

There is something more to add about the words "Tampico" and "San Antonio, Texas." When we were children, my brothers and I used a language all our own in play. Instead of "sí" we would say "sirilo" and instead of "no," "norolo". Of course Don Justo was aware of our informal home-language. This allows us to shed a little more light on his autobiography. Our word for "tampoco" was "tampico." The adverb "tampoco," in Spanish, serves like the English word "nor," to introduce the second of two negative clauses of the form, "neither... nor." I sincerely believe that in using the word "tampico," Don Justo deliberately intended to suggest the Spanish, "tampoco."

When he writes, "in infancy or childhood I found myself in San Antonio, Texas when it belonged to México,... and afterwards, while still a minor, I found myself in "Tampico," it is to suggest, as I see it, two consecutive negations: first, that the place where he found himself in infancy or childhood was not "San Antonio, Texas" (it was Austria); and second, that the place where he later found himself was not "Tampico" either (it was Argentina).

So all the details of his autobiography were written with great deliberation, in order that the truth about his life and who he was might be revealed when the time came. After much thought I have considered proper to publish these facts, over forty years after his death, and to reveal the intimate details of one of the most fascinating and strange mysteries of recent history. He kept his promise not to reveal his identity, but I am free to write what I know to be true. I do so out of respect and love for his memory.

g) He chose to mention the year 1860 because that year saw a decisive change in his home, as we shall discuss later. And in that same document he tells us that in 1930 he was ninety-one. In that case he would have been born in 1839; and had he arrived in El Salvador in 1860, as he says in his autobiography, he would then have been twenty-one.

But all this, taken literally, is false. He was born on August 21, 1858. He arrived in El Salvador in September 1898, at the age of forty, and not at the age of twenty-one, as he suggested by claiming to be ninety-one in 1930, and to have arrived in El Salvador in 1860. The only purpose of this evident falsehood is to tell us two things of great importance: first, that the year 1860 was critical in his life; and second, that in his judgement, his arrival in El Salvador and his hearing the tragic news of his mother's death marked his having reached the age of manhood, the classical twenty-first year. In effect, from the time he arrived in El Salvador, the Archduke was a grown man, both from the economic and, above all, spiritual point of view.

This completes the sum of the information that he gives us in his autobiography on the stages of his life.

h) The Archduke was a genius whose presence was fascinating. Kings, princes, and rulers everywhere in Europe praised him for his presence, the maturity of his thought, and his clear understanding of political problems. But something was still missing. His impetuous and innovative spirit still suffered from a lack of respect for traditional values, and from the consequent lack of prudence. His enemies took advantage of these defects. And his enemies were no less than the Jesuits and Ministers Taaffe and Kalnoky.

When the Archduke arrived in El Salvador, the news that his mother had been assassinated threw him into unspeakable agitation. He managed to preserve enough poise to avoid revealing his thoughts and emotions, and to keep his true identity hid. He still lacked this capacity to conceal his thoughts and emotions when he was in Austria. And that is why he tells us that at the time, when in Austria, he was still in his nonage or childhood. But from the time of his arrival in El Salvador, when he finally succeeded in preserving his serenity in the most tragic moment of his life, he felt that he had become an adult, having reached the symbolic twenty-one years.

i) If we may go over the autobiography again, the Archduke tells us the following:

First, that in his judgement, while he lived in Austria he was still in his nonage or childhood. In reality, he was a child in the midst of many astute experts in political maneuvers and intrigue.

Second, that when he lived in Argentina in the care of a Spanish family, he still felt himself a minor. He remembers that family gratefully, and as one of noble sentiments, as he suggests by preceding the name *Armas* with the preposition *de*, which he thinks befits them. By these means he also indicates that he is no commoner, but of noble birth, *de* Armas, *von* Habsburg.

And third, that on arrival in El Salvador, where he succeeded in providing for himself and in thinking freely, without political preoccupations and without the strict traditions of his family, he felt that he had finally reached manhood, and with it true and complete spiritual maturity.

His arrival in El Salvador was an emotional cataclysm. But it was above all a constructive cataclysm. An entire past was shed, and an entire future began to open up.

j) We have said that the year 1860 marked a decisive change in the Archduke's home. In that year, the Empress Elizabeth was denied any further participation in the upbringing of her children, and especially of the Crown Prince. In despair, she thereafter spent much of her time away from the household, sometimes for years in succession. Generally she went to Madeira or the Mediterranean.

This change in family relationships (when at the age of two he was removed entirely from his mother's attentions and placed under the care of harsh preceptors), engraved itself in the Archduke's memory, and so he included that specific date of 1860 in his autobiography. He knew that no one would seriously take that as the date of his arrival in El Salvador. He simply wanted to tell us that was a tragic date in his life.

This date marked the partial separation from his mother, and his being placed in the hands of tutors. His arrival in El Salvador marked the total separation from his mother, for in that year she was assassinated by the shores of Lake Geneva. And it marked the total separation from his motherland. Now it was necessary to forget the past.

The association of ideas is clear between 1860, his separation from his mother, her assassination, his arrival in El Salvador, and his effort to forget the unending tragedy of his life in his motherland. When he wrote in his autobiography, "that in 1860 I came in this Republic El Salvador," the Archduke tells us two important facts:

First, "the year in which they assassinated my mother, I came to this Republic." We have explained the association of ideas linking the year 1860 to his total separation from both his mother, Empress Elizabeth, and his motherland.

Second, by writing "República El Salvador" and not "República de El Salvador" (which is the correct form), he indicates that he is using *El Salvador* in another sense. In Spanish, *El Salvador* means "The Saviour."

In brief, what the Archduke wished to say in his autobiography is "that in the year in which they assassinated my mother I came to this Republic, which has indeed been *the saviour* to me." The Archduke is quite right. After suffering so many tragedies, his arrival in El Salvador was indeed *his salvation*.

Beyond The Grave

ow that we have analyzed the life of Archduke Rudolf, it is natural to speculate on what would have happened if Mayerling had never occurred.

It might well have been possible that the Emperor Francis Joseph, in view of the complicated European political situation, would have decided to abdicate in favor of his son, Archduke Rudolf (as Emperor Ferdinand I had abdicated in 1848 in favor of his nephew the young Archduke Francis Joseph). But because of the collusion of the clergy and the ultraconservatives of the Empire, the Archduke disappeared from the Austrian political scene in 1889.

The Archduke lost the opportunity to become Emperor, but got the opportunity to triumph over the powerful forces of those who wanted to imprison him in a monastery for the rest of his life. And he got the opportunity to struggle against the adverse powers of violent storms and waves at freezing temperatures, and come out victorious. And he got the opportunity to actualize to the maximum his reserves of sacred psychic energies during his life in remote regions of Argentina.

From then on Archduke Rudolf was a spiritual giant. His convincing speech and penetrating gaze spread his thoughts abroad over great distances, far outwards, very far in time and space. Thanks to his tempestuous life, thanks to the difficult circumstances that he learned how to rise above in triumph, the Archduke went much further along the path of his personal development, than if he had remained in Austria solving the problems of the Empire. Once the tragedy of Mayerling was over, he managed to solve many quite difficult problems. The most important of all was the actualization of his latent reserves of sacred psychic energies. This is a victory from which there is no retreat, and thereafter that is carried on from incarnation to incarnation.

Many believe it a great happiness and a high honor to gird the brow with the imperial crown. Doubtless it is. What few know is that the imperial crown, however great the honor it confers, is a crown of thorns. Whoever assumes the crown bears it with dignity and never shows his sufferings.

Nevertheless, there are moments of excessive tragedy, like that in which His Majesty the Emperor Francis Joseph was seen to weep freely, because his son was going into perpetual exile. No doubt that on many occasions, being alone and with no one watching, his eyes filled with tears, as when he knew that his wife the Empress Elizabeth had died under an anarchist's knife. And likely when it was thought that the Archduke Rudolf and Archduke Johann Salvator had perished in the Straits of Magellan. And when he received a report clarifying that his son, still the Crown Prince, who had lost the title through no fault of his own (although he had not perished in the shipwreck), walked barefoot in a distant land. And when he was informed that his nephew the Archduke Franz Ferdinand had perished at Sarajevo. And when, at the outbreak of the First World War, he understood too late all the disastrous consequences that war would bring, and that they could have been avoided, at least in part, had the reforms that his son envisaged ever been implemented.

The imperial crown is a constant conflict between public duties on the one hand and personal interests and family affections on the other. Surely the imperial crown, however dazzling, is a crown of thorns. Archduke Rudolf, the Crown Prince, never became Emperor of Austria. But I feel that on thinking by himself, musing on the disappointments of his tempestuous life, he must have arrived at the conclusion that for his own good and personal happiness, given his total spiritual development, it was best to have come to El Salvador and to have lived in my country for the rest of his life.

The Prince knew by his own experience and the remembrance of his past lives, that life does not begin when we are born nor end when we die. Many other lives await us beyond the tomb. All that we learn in a life by means of suffering, by means of all the sequence of hardships and disappointments that we manage to overcome, provide us with a background for our activities in the following incarnation. It is not possible to achieve in only one life the full development of our individual being. Very, very numerous are the incarnations that highly developed spirits have gone through. And many are the lives that they have yet to live.

One should meditate on the four following considerations on our triumphs and failures, for they are the fount of our felicity and our misfortune. 1) On what we have done, when it was the best to have done in view of the circumstances. 2) On what we did and ought not to have done. 3) On what we did not and should have done. And 4) On what we decided not to do because it ought not to be done. It is of the highest importance to follow divine inspiration and to resist temptation. These meditations prepare us to live a happier and more fruitful life in our next incarnation.

Looking backwards, meditating on the gains and understanding bestowed by his experience whether fortunate or otherwise, the Crown Prince doubtless dedicated many hours of his last years in planning what he would do thereafter. In spirit and in his presence the Archduke continued to be the Crown Prince, and forever, in all coming centuries, he will continue to be the Crown Prince or the Emperor, as circumstances might dictate.

Through his experience and all the sufferings inflicted on him during this incarnation, the Prince came to know fully and at first hand the treacherous forces of evil. From now on and through the centuries he will recognize them and prevent and uproot perfidy, even when they appear dissimulated and disguised in the robes of loyalty, friendship, love, and good intentions.

Although his career had been interrupted, he understood that it had been only temporarily checked, because he was determined as always to go forward, and ever forward. To see him standing, looking towards the distant horizon with his hands clasped behind his back, it would have been easy to guess his thoughts and his determination:

"ONCE I COME TO BE BORN AGAIN...."

ADDENDUM

Because of the extraordinary nature of the document and the rarity of expressions and ideas therein contained, we have thought best to reproduce Don Justo's autobiography exactly as he wrote it:

Tengo 91 años de edad (en el año 1930). Nunca he sabido el nombre de mis padres, ni el lugar donde nací, pero recuerdo que durante mi infancia o niñez me hallaba en San Antonio de Texas cuando pertenecía a México, al cuidado de una señora y un sacerdote austriaco, del poder de quienes fui sustraído por unos indios, y posteriormente, todavía en la menor edad me encontré en Tampico, bajo el amparo de una familia española hacendada y muy rica que se apellidaba "de Armas", familia que cariñosamente me atendía y me dio el nombre y apellido que llevo dicho. Que durante mi juventud, siempre me vi provisto de los indispensables recursos para vivir, siempre sin saber de cierto de donde procedían, hasta que con mi personal trabajo pude proporcionármelos. Que el año 1860 vine a esta República El Salvador. Desde entonces soy domiciliado en esta Capital.